S0-BMS-470

The Preschool Letters And Notes To Parents Book

Kathy Charner
Editor

gryphon house®
Mt. Rainier, Maryland, USA

This publication is designed to provide accurate and authoritative information in regard to the subject matter covered. It is sold with the understanding that the publisher is not engaged in rendering legal, accounting, or other professional service. If legal advice or other expert assistance is required, the services of a competent, professional person should be sought.

© Gryphon House, Inc., 1989

ISBN 0-87659-120-9

Library of Congress Catalog Card Number: 89-84578

All rights reserved. No part of this publication may be reproduced, stored in a retrieval system, or transmitted in any form or by any means without written permission of the publisher. Except that educators, teachers and administrators are hereby granted unlimited rights to copy and reproduce contents for use as letters and communications.

The contents of this book are also available
in floppy disk format, as
The Preschool Letters And Notes To Parents Disk,
also published by Gryphon House.

Gryphon House, Inc.
P. O. Box 275
Mt. Rainier MD 20712
1-(800)-638-0928

Printed in the United States of America

Text design: Chip's Graphics
Cover design: Graves, Fowler and Associates

Table of Contents

Introduction

Chapter 1 - Administrative Forms and Notes

Chapter 2 - Health and Safety

Chapter 3 - Brochures

Chapter 4 - Parents and Teachers Working Together

Chapter 5 - Love and Discipline

Chapter 6 - Play and Learning

Chapter 7 - Birthdays, Holidays, and Special Days

Chapter 8 - "Help Wanted"

Introduction

Teachers spend the day teaching loving, helping, singing, educating, enjoying, painting, and reading. At the same time, a lot of information needs to be communicated to the parents. There is not always time to devote to all the forms, notes, letters and reminders that need to be written. This book solves that problem. These are tried-and-true, successful, notes, letters and forms used by schools and day care centers to communicate with parents. They are the winning entries in a national contest for parent notes from early childhood educators.

How To Use This Book

Now that you have a letter for every occasion, how can you be sure that the letter will be read? The communication will only be complete if the parent reads the letter. The following are a few tricks and techniques to catch the attention of the readers and to increase the possibility that the letters will get read.

Use a different color of paper for each type of letter. For example, blue for administrative letters, yellow for teacher-generated notes and red for urgent messages. Change the color for all notes when the season changes, or use a combination of the two methods. Whatever you decide, the change or difference will catch the reader's attention.

Try These Practical Ideas

Using standard size is effective for many notes, but others get noticed if they are written on smaller or larger size paper. Here again, it is the difference that the reader will notice. Even small papers attached by tape or a pin to a backpack or coat can be effective. Or cut paper into a shape that relates to the message. A tooth for a letter about teething, a cake for a birthday message, a book for National Library Week, a pizza for pizza night, or a pumpkin for Halloween.

Graphics that relate to the subject matter in the letter capture the reader's attention. Whether a picture is drawn or photocopied, it adds interest to the letter, and draws attention to it. What the picture accomplishes is to make a letter different. Pictures drawn by hand have a charm and individuality that are hard to ignore.

Using **bold face type**, underlining and ALL CAPITALS draws attention to the critical parts of a note. These sections jump out of the text as if to say, "Read me!" Every letter should look a little different so that people do not think that they have read it before. Use short paragraphs, group material into sections and delineate and define sections. Title headings will tell the reader what they are about to read.

Who Signs The Letter?

For most notes, it is obvious who will sign it, teachers sign teacher-generated notes and administrators sign their notes. But for letters about a serious situation such as late fees or missing information on a medical form, having both sign the letter gives it added importance.

In addition, if subsequent letters are needed to follow up an initial request, having a different person sign each subsequent letter can be effective. For example, first the teacher signs it, then the administrator, then a Board member, then the Chair of the Board.

Now that communication with parents has been simplified, it's time to get back to what is important — the children.

Chapter One

Administrative
Forms
and
Notes

Application For Admission and Contract

Child's Name_____ Known As_____

Sex_____ Age_____ Date Of Birth_____ Home Phone_____

Home Address_____Zip_____

Name of Mother_____ Occupation_____

Employer_____ Business Phone_____

Business Address_____

Name of Father_____ Occupation_____

Employer_____ Business Phone_____

Business Address_____

Person(s) With Legal Custody of Child (relationship) _____

Name of Child's Physician _____Phone_____

Name of Hospital Preferred _____

Person to contact when parents cannot be reached _____

Home Phone_____ Work Phone_____

Relationship to Child _____

Person(s) authorized to pick up child _____

Person(s) **NOT** authorized to visit or pick up child _____

Give name of other school child attends _____

Other people in household (indicate relationship; e.g., brother, grandmother, etc.)

Name	Relationship	Age

In order to assure that new parents clearly understand the procedures and policies of the Center, we ask all parents to read the policies enclosed with the application packet and also to check off the following important items:

_____1. Parents are responsible for payment of fees on time.   A late fee of $10 will be added to bills not paid within two (2) days of the due date.

_____2. There is no reduction of fees for absences or vacations except in the case of an extended illness of the child. The director should be notified if such a situation occurs.

3. I understand that:

_____a) I must walk into the building with my child each day and make certain the teacher knows he/she is there.   Older siblings are not to bring or pick up children.

_____b) I, or a responsible *designated* adult, will walk into the building to pick up my child(ren) and inform a teacher that we are leaving.

_____4. I give my consent for my child(ren) to ride on public transportation or the Center's school bus to go on field trips.

_____5. Keep children home with the following: those with fever, diarrhea or vomiting in previous 24-hour period. Children too sick to participate in full program, including outside play, need to be kept at home.

_____6. All preschool & kindergarten children need a complete change of clothing and a blanket at the Center at all times, with the child's name on each item.

_____7. Parents need to inform the Center of changes in addresses, phone number, employment, emergency information or any changes in family situations.

_____8. Parent is expected to pick up children before closing time, _____ p.m. There will be an overtime charge of $_____ for each 15 minutes or portion thereof after _____ p.m.

_____9. No medication can be administered to a child without written consent and instructions from the doctor.

_____10. The director is to be notified TWO WEEKS IN ADVANCE before a child is to be withdrawn. Parents are required to pay for those two weeks regardless of when the child leaves the Center.

_____11. If, after a reasonable period of time, it is found that a child is unable to adjust to the Center, the Center reserves the right to request withdrawal of child. This decision is left to the discretion of the Director(s).

_____12. I agree to abide by these rules and regulations .

Date_____ Signature of Parent or Guardian _____

Pam Humphrey, Takoma Park Day Care Center, Takoma Park MD

Schedule Of Care

Please Schedule _____   Age_____

Beginning_____
              Date of desired entrance

For the following times weekly: (List the child's approximate arrival and departure times)

                    Arrival   Departure

Monday _____ to _____

Tuesday_____ to _____

Wednesday_____ to _____

Thursday_____ to _____

Friday _____ to _____

_____

Date Billing Began_____ Date Of Withdrawal_____

Parent's Signature _____

Director's Signature _____

Pam Humphrey, Takoma Park Day Care Center, Takoma Park MD

Registration Agreement

We have reserved a place for your child, _____, for the school year beginning _____, 19__.

Tuition is $_____ for the entire year. Tuition may be paid in one lump sum, or in ten monthly installments of $_____ . The first installment is due at the time of registration, there after payable by the 15th of each month starting with _____ 15, and ending _____ 15. If payment is received after the 15th day of the month, the family will be charged a $_____ late fee. **Payment by check is preferred**. Returned checks will be surcharged a $_____ bank processing fee.

Monthly payment $_____.

Payment Option: Tuition may be paid in thirds:

September 15th _____

December 15th _____

March 15th _____

Thirty days written notice must be given to the school if a child is to withdraw from enrollment. Parents are responsible for each month's tuition, in spite of absences. The school's budget and teacher's salaries are based upon full enrollment, therefore, compensation cannot be given for absences.

We reserve the right to enforce a tardiness fee for families who are habitually late at dismissal time. If our dismissal time is a problem, please speak to the director.

_____   _____

Signature of both parents

Or

_____

Guardian

Date_____

Margaret Adams, The Presbyterian Nursery School on the Green, Bloomfield NJ

Initial Parent Conference

Parent's Name _____

Child's Name _____

Birth: Normal _____ Premature _____ Overdue _____ Caesarian ____
Complication _____ (e.g.,Toxemia or other complication) Birth Weight _____
Serious illness or hospitalization? Yes____ No____ Describe_____
_____
Is child currently taking medication? Yes ____ No ____ Describe
_____

_____

Has child had previous preschool experience? ____ When _____
Where_____
Is there anything about your child's behavior that concerns you? (at home or at school?)
Describe_____
_____

Family Information

Mother:
   High School Attended_____
   College Attended_____ Certificate/degree? _____
   Attending School Now? No____ Yes____
   Occupation: Present _____
            Former_____
            Future Plans: (School, Work, etc.) _____

Father:
   High School Attended_____
   College Attended _____ Certificate/degree? _____
   Attending School Now? No____ Yes____
   Occupation: Present_____
            Former_____
            Future Plans: (School, Work, etc.)_____

_____

Siblings: Name	Sex	Age	Name	Sex	Age
_____	____	____	_____	____	____
_____	____	____	_____	____	____
_____	____	____	_____	____	____

Eating Habits:

How many meals each day does your family eat together?_____

How would you describe child's appetite?_____

What is your child's best meal? Breakfast _____ Lunch _____ Dinner _____ Snacks _____

What or who is your primary source of information for nutritional information?

_____

Bedtime Habits:

Awakens at _____a.m.   Naps: Yes_____ No_____   Goes To Bed At _____p.m.

Does child sleep through the night? yes_____ no_____

Explain:_____

_____

_____

Does child sleep alone _____ In own bed _____ In own room _____

Does child remain dry throughout the night? yes_____ no_____ (if no, please explain)

_____

_____

Parenting

What method of discipline is most effective with your child?

_____

_____

How do you see yourself in parenting role? (percent of time)

Permissive_____ Disciplinarian_____ Consistent _____ Hesitant _____

Other_____

How do you see spouse in parenting role? (percent of time)

Permissive_____ Disciplinarian_____ Consistent _____ Hesitant _____

Other_____

Why do you wish to enroll your child at_____

_____

_____

Additional Comments: _____

_____

_____

Nancy Liggett, Long Beach City College, Child Study Center, Pacific Coast Campus, Long Beach CA

Fall Orientation Meeting

Dear Parents,

This is just a reminder that the fall orientation meeting is scheduled for
_____, 19___ at _____. We will meet in _____.
It would be helpful if you bring your Parent's Handbook with you that day.

Please plan on attending this meeting without your child so we may familiarize you with
our program. This meeting should last about an hour and a half.

There will be a children's open house on _____, 19___ from
_____to _____. This is specifically for new children to come and visit their school.

Barbara Kohler, Pierce College, The Children's Center, Tacoma, WA

Missing Information

Dear _____:

In order to comply with state regulations, we need the following information for our files
as soon as possible. This information is important and must be in our files if we are continued
to be licensed. Thank you for your cooperation.

Sincerely,

Information Needed:_____

_____

_____

_____

Linda Moon, Salvation Army Blue Valley Day Care, Kansas City MO

Field Trip Procedure

Permission slips for each field trip will be sent home with the children. Permission slips must be signed and returned **promptly.** Children without signed permission slips will not be able to go on the scheduled field trip.

Field trips will be posted on the calendar outside the classroom. You are responsible for checking the calendar when you bring your child to school. Individual notification about field trips is impossible. If you do not wish to have your child participate in a trip, please keep him/her home on the appropriate day, and notify the teacher that you are doing so.

The driving parents will follow the route designated by the teachers and drive in a caravan to and from school.

_____adheres to the state seat belt law on all field trips. Therefore, in accordance with the law, all children, when being transported on field trips, will not ride in the front seat, will be belted individually and will not use a shoulder restraint.

Cathy Griffin, Dutch Neck Presbyterian Cooperative Nursety School, Princeton Junction, NJ

Field Trip Consent Form

On _____, the

children from _____ will be taking a field trip.

Where:_____

Time:_____

Cost:_____

My child: _____(Circle) Will be attending   Will *Not* be attending

I can chaperone _____ I cannot chaperone _____

Signed _____ Date _____

Please return to your child's teacher by _____

Dee Balsis, Academy of Preschool Learning, South Milwaukee WI

Individuals Permitted To Pick Up Child(ren)

Dear Parents,

       In accordance with the state law we must have on file the names, addresses and telephone numbers of the individuals permitted to drop off and collect your child(ren) from our school. If someone arrives to collect your child(ren) and we have not been introduced and their name is not in our file we **CANNOT** allow your child to leave with them.

       Please list below any person's name, address and telephone number who **might** arrive to collect your child, so that we can avoid any embarassment, inconvenience or, heaven forbid, tragedy. Also, please call us if your child will not be in attendance.

       Thank you for your cooperation.

Do not detach. Return to school as soon as possible.

_____ may be delivered or collected from school by the following adults:

_____

_____

_____

_____

I understand that if the name does not appear on this list, my child will not be released from school.

_____
Parent's Signature

_____
Date

Margaret Adams, The Presbyterian Nursery School on the Green, Bloomfield NJ

Application For Tuition Aid

The monies available for tuition aid are limited. The school has no endowment, so that whatever funds are available come from individuals or groups who contribute specifically for this purpose. It is because of this situation that application for tuition aid must be made. To receive consideration for tuition aid, you should provide the following information together with any other pertinent information you may wish to submit. Also, a recent stub from a paycheck, or other verification of income, must be attached. These should be submitted by _____, 19__. After receipt and review of the tuition aid application, you will be informed of the financial arrangements.

Name of Child _____ Birth Date _____

Home Address _____ ZIP _____ Phone _____

Name of Father _____

Address _____ ZIP_____ Phone _____

Name of Mother _____

Employer_____

Address _____ ZIP _____ Phone _____

Number of adults in household _____ Number employed _____ Number of children _____

Total family income last year before taxes $_____

Total Family income anticipated this year $_____

Class child attends (or will enter)_____ Number of days child attends _____

Please state the circumstances in the family that should be taken into consideration as this tuition aid application is evaluated.

_____

_____

_____

_____

Signature Of Mother   Date   Signature Of Father   Date

Margaret Adams, The Presbyterian Nursery School on the Green, Bloomfield NJ

Walking Field Trips Permission

I give my permission for my child _____
                                     (First)   (Last)

to participate in walking trips throughout the school year (summer included) when planned by the staff as a regular part of the children's program/curriculum.

I understand that no such trip will be undertaken unless a safe ration of adults to children exists and that no trip will exceed one-half mile (to destination and return to the Center).

Children will not leave on walking trips before 9:00 a.m. or 1:00 p.m. and will have returned by 11:15 a.m. or 3:15 p.m. Announcements of walking trips will be posted on the sign-in clipboard on the day of the trip or before.

Date_____   Parent's Signature _____

Nancy Liggett, Long Beach City College, Child Study Center, Pacific Coast Campus, Long Beach, CA

Permission To Communicate About Child

I, _____, give the staff of _____

and the staff of _____ permission to

communicate fully regarding my child, _____

Parent Signature_____ Date _____

Pam Humphrey, Takoma Park Day Care Center, Takoma Park MD

School Year Bits And Pieces

This school year is well under way and we are having lots of fun learning through play and some additional structured activities. We have learned that it is fun to be growing and gaining the ability to accomplish new tasks. One of our major goals for this year is developing the awareness that everyone in our world is important and that everyone has feelings and needs.

We have several items that we feel that you should make note of, and, hopefully, will help us keep things moving smoothly in the Center:

1. Preschool tuition is to be paid weekly or biweekly. Those parents who do not keep their child's tuition up-to-date will be terminated with no option for re-enrolling the child. All fees must be paid by check or money order.

2. Please bring your child(ren) into the building each morning. No child should ever enter the building in the morning without being with an adult.

3. Children should always be dressed appropriately for the weather. Always label your child's clothing and other items the child will be bringing to school.

4. If your child is ill and will not be attending the Center on any given day, please call your child's teacher at the Center.

5. If your child is going home with another child in the Center or being picked up by someone else, please inform the child's teacher and make certain that you have filled out the necessary consent release form.

6. Several children have asked about bringing things from home to share. The policy is yes, but only on Fridays. Please make sure it is something which won't break easily or with small pieces that will get lost. "Share and Tell Day" is every Friday.

7. The children may bring cookies or cupcakes for a snack on their birthday. However, please inform the teacher before the day of the party.

8. Parents are always welcome to visit the Center. If parents wish to volunteer time in the Center, call and establish a date with your child's teacher.

9. If you have any major concerns, please address them to your child's teacher or call the office at _____-_____.

Herman E. Walston, Ky State University, Rosenwald Center for Early Childhood Development, Frankfort KY

Just A Few Words About

Clothing .

Be sure that your child's clothing

- Is comfortable, washable, and allows for self-dressing,
- Is marked with child's name,
- Is appropriate for arts and crafts (paint smocks are provided).

We get *involved* in activities and should not have to be overly concerned with staying clean. Dresses with ruffles and bows and pants with difficult belts and fastenings should be avoided.

When the weather is cold, always:

- Send in mittens, hat, and a sweater to layer over clothes (Classrooms are warm, often an undershirt and shirt are warm enough for indoors) We do go out most days.
- Have your child carry in snowpants and boots (we will help to put them on), rather than wear them in the car on the way to school and spend precious time taking them off.
- Remember that boots can be difficult to put on over some shoes — please provide plastic bags to put over shoes before putting on boots.
- Remember that shoe boots become *so* warm if worn all day — please send in slippers or alternate shoes for indoors.
- Provide pants for girls who wear dresses with tights — those little legs get *so* cold without extra protection!

When it rains, always:

- Send in a raincoat
- Please leave umbrellas AT HOME!

Safety

Umbrellas are unsafe in a group of children — they ***are not*** allowed!

Jelly shoes do not stay on feet at all times, do not provide enough traction on steps, ladders, or tricycles — they ***are not*** allowed!

Toys

Guns, swords and toys that could hurt another child ***are not*** allowed! They will be taken away and put aside until dismissal — so why not keep them home.

Cartoon-inspired toys (He-Man, My Little Pony, etc.) encourage specific sorts of play. They keep children from the open-ended activities which we offer and from the excellent equipment we provide. Help your child to learn to leave these toys at home!

Thank you for your cooperation.

Walking Child(ren) Into Building

Dear Parents,

It is very important for you to accompany your children to their classroom when they arrive at the center. The reasons for this are:

1. The teachers have no way of knowing that the child has entered the building, therefore they are unsupervised in the hallway.

2. There is an attendance sheet outside (inside for school age children) their classroom. The parents must check the child in so that you know that we know they are here: transfer of responsibility.

3. It gives the parents a chance to "share" the Center with their children. They spend many hours here every day, five days a week. It is important for them to have time to show you their friends, the materials and equipment they work with, and to see you making contact with their teachers.

It is equally important for you to enter the Center at the end of the day when you pick up the children, for many of the same reasons. And some others:

1. If someone else is dropping off or picking up your child, they must follow the same procedures to check the children out so we know you have resumed responsibility for them.

2. To check their cubbies for art work and any messages or notices we have for you (like this one),

Thanks for your cooperation.

Sincerely,

Pam Humphrey, Takoma Park Day Care Center, Takoma Park MD

Late Pick-up

Dear Parents,

We have a serious problem. Closing time at the Center is _____ p.m. All the staff expects to be able to leave work at that time, just as you expect to leave your job at your scheduled time.

We understand that **occasionally** you are delayed beyond your control. However, with so many families at the Center, if a different family comes late each day and each family is late only five times during the year, our staff would be required to stay late every day. As a result, none of our staff wants to work past _____ p.m. The late fee does not compensate for making *us* late for the commitments we have after _____ p.m. (caring for our own children, getting to classes on time, etc.).

Because of this situation, if you are a **frequent** late parent, you will receive a letter telling you of additional penalties and eventually termination. You will also be asked to sign the late book each time you pick up after _____ p.m.

There is another issue you can help us with. If you arrive a few minutes before _____ p.m., please do not involve the classroom or office staff in lengthy conversations. As much as we want to discuss issues of concern we also want to leave work on time. You are encouraged to call the Center anytime for the office staff; call between _____ and _____ to speak with the teachers.

Thank you for your cooperation.

Pam Humphrey, Takoma Park Day Care Center, Takoma Park MD

Late Pick-up Fees

There will be a $_____ late fee for parents failing to pick up their child(ren) by _____ for the morning session and _____ at the end of the day. After _____ in the afternoon or _____ at the end of the day, there will be an additional $_____ charge for every 15 minute period therafter.

Late pick-up causes hardship for staff and cannot be condoned. Repeated lateness will result in suspension.

Late-fee money is given directly to the teacher who supervised your child while waiting for pick-up. Late-fee money is due the following day. Checks may be made out directly to the teacher.

Judy Nygren, Clara Barton Center for Children, Bethesda, MD

Late Payment

Dear_____   Date_____

Your payment of $_____ was due on _____.

Your are now _____ late. If you do not pay $_____ by_____ your child will **not** be able to attend the Center as of _____ and until your payment is received.

Please abide by the rules and regulations of the Center. Failure to do so can result in termination of care.

Thank you for your immediate attention to this matter.

Pam Humphrey, Takoma Park Day Care Center, Takoma Park MD

Reminder Of Pick-up Names

Dear Parents,

When you enrolled at the Center we asked you to indicate who would pick up your child. It is very important for your child's safety and welfare that we and the child be aware of any changes that might occur. A brief note or telephone call to inform us of a "special" pick-up is necessary. If a relative, friend or neighbor is replacing the regular pick-up person — if only for one day — **we must know** who that will be. It would be advisable to let your child know in advance also, if possible.

We will not release your child to anyone unless you have given us permission to do so. If your child remains at the Center after _____ p.m. because you did not tell us of a pick-up change, you will be responsible for a late fee.

Please keep us informed of any changes of your regular pick-up people. Thank you for your cooperation.

Pam Humphrey, Takoma Park Day Care Center, Takoma Park, MD

Frequent Late Pick-ups

Dear _____,

Our records show that you have **frequently** been arriving after _____ to pick up your child. As stated in a previous letter on this subject, it is very inconvenient for our staff to work after _____. The next time you are late the fee will increase to $_____ for every fifteen minutes or portion thereof, **to be paid promptly**. The staff would rather leave work on time than receive the late fee money. However, compensation is needed for working above and beyond the call of duty.

If you are late again after that, the late fee is still $_____. In addition, your child will **not** be able to attend the Center for the next day. A late pick-up after this will result in termination of care.

We do not want to have to terminate care for your child; it is not in the best interest of the child. You knew the Center closes at _____ when you enrolled your child. Please accept your responsibilities to your child and the Center.

Thank you for cooperating.

Pam Humphrey, Takoma Park Day Care Center, Takoma Park MD

Reminder Of Fees, Pick-ups And Vacations

Dear Parents:

It's "reminder" time again.

(1) Late pick-up. We realize circumstances can cause us to run late from time to time, but we do need to try to pick up our children by the regular closing time of _____ p.m. A telephone call will let us know if you are running late. A late pick-up fee of $_____ is charged for any portion of the first 15 minutes and $_____ for each additional ___ minutes.

(2) Payment of fees. Fees can be paid weekly, monthly or every two weeks — whichever is most convenient. All we ask is that they are paid no later than _____. Here again, we do realize circumstances can cause problems from time to time, and we are more than willing to help work out satisfactory arrangements. We also ask that you be conscientious in letting us know if you are having a problem. Fees should not get more than two weeks in arrears.

We have been very lenient to overlook charging late fees on payments and late pick-ups. You are very important to us and we want to be sensitive to your concerns with time and money.

(3) Absence and vacation time. After a child has been attending the Center a year, they are entitled to two weeks vacation time, no charge. But if a parent chooses to take their child out for a day or two now and then, regular fees are charged. We also charge regular fees when a child is ill unless the illness is one that requires hospitalization and the child will be absent a week or more. But as in any situation, there can be extenuating circumstances in this area as well. You are welcome to talk to the director about the possibility of a reduced fee for serious illness.

If you have any questions, please stop by the office.

Ruth Ann Ball, Rose State College Child Development Program, Midwest City OK

Winter Weather Reminders

Dear Parents:

We are into the snow and ice season. Please remember the following:

1. Listen to radio station _____ for school closings.

2. We will open the doors as soon as the first staff person is able to get here, which will be as close to _____ a.m. as possible.

3. If bad weather develops during the day, please make arrangements to leave work early. We don't want children and staff stranded at the Center. Late fees for pick-up are in effect regardless of weather or traffic conditions.

4. If we call you during the day to say that the Center is closing early due to serious weather conditions, **you need to pick up your child by the designated time.**

5. We take the children out to play in the snow. Please send your child with snow pants, boots, hat, mittens and a warm jacket. The bag of extra clothes is important in case clothing gets wet.

Pam Humphrey, Takoma Park Day Care Center, Takoma Park, MD

Warm Weather Reminders

Dear Parents,

Warm weather has arrived. You need to check your child's bag of clothing: lightweight shirts and pants (shorts) should replace winter clothing. Please make sure you always have underwear and socks in the bag.

Children must wear tennis shoes (or other closed-toe shoes): Absolutely **no** sandals, flip flops or jellies, for safety reasons. Please have your child wear socks each day.

It is also time to take home your child's winter "nap time" blanket and send in a lightweight cover. Take it home periodically to be washed.

Remember, label **everything** with your child's name.

Thanks for your cooperation.

Pam Humphrey, Takoma Park Day Care Center, Takoma Park MD

Re-enrollment Letter

Dear Parents,

     Many of you are planning to withdraw your children sometime during this summer. Current kindergarten children will be eligible to remain at our center through August, but some of you may have plans to leave before that date. Others with younger children may also plan to terminate before September. I would like to have as accurate a picture as possible of when the openings will occur in order to notify the families on our waiting list. **Please fill out the form below and return it by _____, 19__.**

     In addition to this notification, we still need a written statement giving us two weeks' notice before you withdraw your child.

_____

Withdrawal

Please check one

( ) I plan to withdraw my child, _____, effective _____.
                                                         date

( ) My child, _____, will not be at the Center next fall but I have not decided   on the date of withdrawal.

( ) I have no plans to withdraw my child, _____

Signature:_____

Date _____

Joyce Stockdill, Silver Spring Child Care Center, Silver Spring MD

Waiting List Opening Letter

Dear _____,

     We have an opening in our _____ session at _____, and _____'s name is next on our waiting list.

     Please read the enclosed materials that explain our goals and philosophy. Class starts on _____, 19__. Tuition is $_____ for the year, billed _____. A deposit of $_____ will hold your place.

     Please call me after you have read this letter (as soon as possible whether or not you plan to enroll your child), and I will schedule an appointment for you to meet with _____, your child's teacher. Then if you wish to bring your child for a visit, we can arrange that as well. I need to hear from you by _____, 19__.

     I look forward to hearing from you. It is important to have a deposit to hold your place. Thank you for your interest in our program.

Barbara Kohler, Pierce College, The Children's Center, Tacoma, WA

Mid-year Opening Letter

Dear _____,

     You asked that I let you know if any of the children dropped out of the _____class here at _____.

     One of the children is dropping out effective _____, 19__. Therefore, if you are still interested, you are next on our list. This class meets on _____ from _____ to _____. The tuition is $_____. The bills are sent monthly.

     If you plan to enroll your child, I would need a deposit of $_____. The deposit is held for your last month's payment.

     Please let me know your decision by _____, 19__. If you want to come by and visit while the children are here, that can be arranged.

Barbara Kohler, Pierce College, The Children's Center, Tacoma WA

Parting Questionnaire

So that we may best serve our children, the Parent Council would appreciate if you would take a few minutes to complete this questionnaire. Please return it directly to the Parent Council President in the stamped envelope provided.

This information will be kept confidential. We are interested in anything that will help us improve the staff and services at _____. We hope that your experience here has been a happy one, but if not please tell us.

Thank you for your time and cooperation.

1. How old is (are) your child(ren) at _____? ____ ____ ____.

2. When did you first enroll your child at _____? year____ month____.

3. Has the quality of the services at _____ changed since then?
   a lot better_____ somewhat better_____ about the same_____.

4. How satisfied overall have you been with your child's care at the Center in the last year?
   very satisfied_____ can't complain_____ somewhat unhappy_____ very unhappy_____

5. Do you feel that the program adequately satisfied your child's needs? highly fulfilling_____
   above average _____ adequate _____ inadequate _____ very inadequate _____

6. How qualified do you feel that the teachers at the Center are?
   highly qualified _____ qualified_____ poorly qualified_____

7. Will you recommend _____ to other parents seeking day care?
   highly recommend_____ recommend with reservations_____ tell them to look elsewhere_____

8. Do you know the Director's name? _____

   Do you feel that the Director runs the Center very well _____ adequately _____ poorly _____

9. How safe and protected do you feel that your child was during his/her time at the Center?
   always very safe_____ usually safe _____ sometimes a little unsafe _____ often unsafe_____

10. How happy has your child been at the Center?
    very happy_____ usually quite happy_____ sometimes unhappy_____ often unhappy_____

11. How well do you feel that the physical space and facilities serve the needs of the children?
    very well _____ adequately _____ somewhat inadequate _____ very inadequate _____

12. How well did the toys and equipment serve your child's needs?
    very well _____ adequately ____ inadequately _____

13. Did the hours of operation suit your needs or should they be changed?
    open earlier_____ just right_____ close later_____ open earlier and close later_____

14. Why are you leaving the Center? _____

_____

15. Any additional comments? _____

_____

You may sign your name if you wish: _____

Chapter Two

Health
and
Safety

Medical Form

Medical form to be completed by doctor and returned to school as soon as possible (please print)

Child's Name _____

Birthdate _____ Height _____ Weight _____

Growth_____
               (normal)   (other)

Eyes — With Glasses _____ Without Glasses_____

Ears — Hearing Loss _____ Other Defects _____

Heart _____ Lungs _____ Tonsils _____

Nose _____ Nutrition _____

Skin_____ Speech_____

Glands_____
         (cervical)   (thyroid)   Other (specify)

Orthopedic — Structural Defects _____ Posture_____

Scoliosis _____ Feet _____ Hernia _____ Blood Pressure _____

Symptoms Of Nervous Disorder _____

Operations_____

Serious Injuries _____

Allergies_____

Recent Immunizations_____

Is there any condition which would limit participation in the physical education program?

_____

_____

Additional Remarks That May Be Of Value To The School_____

_____

_____
Name of physician (please print)

_____   _____
Signature of physician   Date

Margaret Gibson-Adams, The Presbyterian Nursery School on the Green, Bloomfield NJ

Vaccine Schedule

Child's name _____

Address _____

_____

Birth date _____

TO BE COMPLETED BY A PHYSICIAN

	Approximate dates (month/year)	
Vaccine type Primary series		Booster shots
Combined (DPT)	_____	_____
Oral Polio vaccine	_____	_____
Measles vaccine	_____	_____
Rubella vaccine	_____	_____
Mumps vaccine	_____	_____
Tuberculin test	_____	_____
Other — specify	_____	_____

Immunizations are incomplete because of:

_____ Medical reasons _____ Religious exemption

_____ Allergies _____

Physical and/or emotional handicaps _____

Signature of physician _____ Date_____

Office address_____Phone_____

This form is to be returned before child is registered for school.

Margaret Gibson-Adams, The Presbyterian Nursery School on the Green, Bloomfield NJ

First Aid Permission & Emergency Informat

Child's Name _____ Age _____

I give _____ permission to administer first aid to my child. In case of emergency, the school staff promptly contacts the parents. If neither the parent nor the emergency phone number can be reached, and in case of surgical emergency, I hereby give permission to the physician selected by the _____ director to hospitalize and secure proper treatment for my child as named above.

Signature _____ (Parent or Guardian)

Date _____

Emergency Information

Parent's Name _____

Address _____

Home Phone _____

Work Phone _____

Family Doctor _____

Phone _____

In case of emergency when neither parent can be reached, please contact

Name _____ Address _____

_____

Phone _____ Relationship To Child _____

Margaret Gibson-Adams, The Presbyterian Nursery School on the Green Bloomfield, NJ

Accident Report

Child's Name _____

Date _____ Time _____

Circle One: Accident Report   Other Medical Report

Explanation:_____

_____

_____

_____

Treatment:_____

_____

_____

Child's Reaction: _____

_____

_____

Follow-up Suggested: _____

_____

Signature Of Attending Staff:_____

Shari Magnin, First United Methodist Preschool, Glendale AZ

Illness Policy

Dear Parents,

Since we are beginning the cold and flu season, we thought it would be a good idea to review our illness policy.

If a child comes to school when he/she is not feeling well, he/she will be more vulnerable to infection. It is in the best interests of your child and of the other people at _____ to keep your child at home when he/she is ill. A child needs to be well to be able to participate actively in the program.

1. After a fever, a child's temperature **must be normal (98.6) for 24 hours before he/she returns to school.**

2. If a child is well enough to come to school, we will expect him/her to go outdoors with his/her class, weather permitting.

3. Often, children may ask to come to school even though they are ill. Although your child may be disappointed, please keep him/her at home if he/she is sick.

4. If your child becomes ill while at school and you are called, please cooperate by picking up your child promptly. We will not call unless your child needs to be at home.

Admitting Children With Infectious Disease

Parents or guardians of any child enrolled in _____ or making application for enrollment must notify the director of any medical condition requiring special attention or consideration. Children afflicted with infectious disease shall be excluded from_____. When the child is free of disease, a physician's note to that effect must be submitted to the director. The child may then be readmitted.

Judy Nygren, Clara Barton Center for Children, Bethesda MD

Teething

Dear Mom and Dad:

Some of us are entering the teething stage of our growth and development. Most of the time it's okay, but there are times when it can be a real pain in the gums.

Teacher has learned a few tricks that can be helpful.

1. Some teething rings are too hard, they can actually hurt more than the teething itself. A wet, cold rough face cloth can be quite soothing.

2. Teacher can use Dr. Hands teething lotion without a note from the doctor because it only contains clove oil, but it really works well.

3. Not warming my bottles too much also helps; keep them on the cool side, if I will accept it.

4. Also, cooler food tastes better now, i.e., fruit, yogurt, maybe even a little Jell-O once in a while.

5. Try real hard to keep me on my regular schedule, I really need my rest and good meal times. If I get tired or hungry, it only makes me feel worse.

We are in for trying times and some sleepless nights, but soon I will be showing off my first pearly whites for friends and family.

Love,

Your Baby

Margaret Dvorak, Old Lyme Daycare, Old Lyme CT

Head Lice

In an effort to control outbreaks of head lice, the Health Department is appealing to parents to be on the lookout for the lice and to take prompt action if their children become infested.

The family physician should be consulted if a child is found to have head lice. Treatment includes the use of medicated shampoo and the disinfecting of personal articles. Fumigation of homes or schools is not recommended.

Although they can spread from person to person, head lice (unlike body lice) do not transmit disease. However, scratching of bites may lead to a secondary bacterial infection.

Head lice thrive only on the hair and scalps of humans and are commonly found at the nape of the neck and behind the ears. Usually, only 10 to 20 are present on a person — although larger infestations have been reported. The lice grow in small grayish-white oval eggs called nits, which attach firmly to the base of hairs.

They spread by direct contact with an infested person or by means of hair brushes, towels, pillow cases, hats, ribbons, and other head coverings used by someone with lice.

When examining a person, the Health Department recommends parting the hair with a wooden applicator stick. Usually head lice and nits can be seen with the naked eye, but a magnifying glass and flashlight can help. Lice are about the size of a pencil point and are most often found behind the ears and at the nape of the neck. Nits are gray white specks resembling dandruff firmly attached to the hairs a few inches from the scalp.

To disinfect personal articles, the Health Department recommends:

- Machine-wash them in hot water and detergent. Dry them at high heat for at least 20 minutes.
- Dry clean any clothing that is not washable.
- Treat combs and brushes with a special medicated shampoo, or soak them for an hour in a 2 percent Lysol solution.
- Vacuum furniture, curtains and rugs and discard bag.
- Eggs and bugs live 48 hours when not on a person.
- Shampoo hair as physician directs you, check again one week later and repeat if necessary.

Pam Humphrey, Takoma Park Day Care Center, Takoma Park MD

We're Nuts About Nutrition

The nutritional needs of preschool children are high because of the relatively high demands of their growth. Their growth rate from infancy slowly decelerates; however, their needs are greater now than in later childhood, though their appetites may seem small.

We always try to be aware of the nutritional value of the food we eat. Our goals are parent involvement and health awareness. We will provide you and your child the opportunity to share and/or prepare a nutritional snack of your choice with us (food or drink).

Some nutrition tips include: using natural sugars, which can be found in fresh fruits and juices, as opposed to Kool-Aid and soft drinks which are either high in sugar or contain minimal nutritional value; using whole grain products, like whole wheat muffins, bran muffins, bran cereal; fresh vegetables and cheeses are also good for us. This is just a beginning into nutritional information, and the list is endless.

The Parent Resource Center will be featuring cookbooks, recipe charts and tips for cooking with your children. We encourage you to take advantage of the display table in the Parent Resource Center.

A sign-up sheet will be located at the Parent table for you to sign when deciding what day you will share your snack. Keep in mind these three options when selecting your day:

1. Your child may bring the ingredients and recipe to be made at school.

2. You and your child may help the children prepare the snack during the school day.

3. You and your child may prepare the snack at home and bring it to school.

We look forward to your nutritional snack!

Lisa Gardner Warner, Child Development Center, Eastern Kentucky University, Richmond KY

Sugar

Dear Parents:

Nutrition is the relationship of foods to the health of the human body. A child needs good nutrition to grow physically, mentally and spiritually.

It is an unfortunate fact that in our society the presence of sugared sweets is all pervasive, and children are taught very early that "candy" (sugared sweets) is "love". Worse, that sweets, ice cream, sugary jams and jellies, sugar coated cereals, are not only good food, but "children's" food.

Much medical research over the past two decades has linked sugar consumption not only with cavities, but also ulcers, heart disease and behavior problems. In the classroom, we have definitely observed behavior changes linked to large sugar consumption.

We are asking for your help. We are not banning sugary foods from the classroom; rather we are limiting the consumption of sugary sweets. Making the best quality food available for our children is of course essential for their future health and well-being.

Rather than focusing on foods to avoid, think instead of adding good quality natural foods. The children will feel satisfied, not deprived, and they'll feel full rather than craving for sugary foods that drag them down. Perhaps foods could include natural unsweetened juices, fruits, raisins, crackers and veggies.

As parents one experiences periods of worry and anxiety about what's best for our children. We hope to turn this around to provide opportunities for growth and discovery. Both teachers and parents want the best for the children.

If you have any questions or suggestions, please feel free to contact any of the teachers.

Jackie Eiche, Jewish Community Center of Atlantic County, Margate NJ

Chapter Three

Brochures

About Our Center

Our center serves the community as a daycare facility and also provides a laboratory setting for college students enrolled in child development classes.

Our main objective is to provide a positive atmosphere which will promote the social, physical, intellectual and emotional growth of children. Learning experiences, appropriate for the developmental age of each group, are provided daily.

Children need to feel good about themselves! Positive guidance techniques are used by our staff to enhance a child's feeling of self-worth. The daily schedule includes breakfast, lunch and an afternoon snack; large and small group interaction which helps the children learn to cooperate, listen and share; self-selected activities which stimulate cognitive growth and creativity, as well as emotional and social development; and outdoor activities which help develop large and small motor skills.

We are professionals. Our staff, as caregivers and teachers of young children, are required to have a minimum of 15 college hours in child development.

Our center is licensed by _____ .

We offer full-time daycare for children three months to five years of age, or until time to start to kindergarten.

Hours Of Operation

Monday — Friday

_____ a.m. to _____ p.m.

Fees

Infants and young toddlers $ _____

1 1/2 to 3 year olds $ _____

3 to 5 year olds $ _____

We do not charge an enrollment or registration fee, but we do require the first and last week's fee at the time of enrollment.

Staff Includes:

Director: _____

Assistant Director: _____

Infant/young Toddler Teachers: _____

1 1/2 To 3 Year Old Teachers: _____

3 Year Old Teachers: _____

4 To 5 Year Old Teachers: _____

Cook: _____

Secretary: _____

In addition to the four regular classrooms for children, our Center has two college classrooms which also serve as observation rooms. Parents are welcome to observe anytime.

A daily report is filled out for each child by the teachers and given to parents at the end of the day. This report tells the parent what activities their child enjoyed, how well they ate and rested, their behavior and other information. Menus are posted in the foyer on the bulletin board and lesson plans are posted by the doorway of each room. A newsletter is sent home once a month advising of upcoming events, birthdays, study themes for the month and other announcements.

Field trips are an integral part of our curriculum. They may include a picnic; a trip to the zoo; three year olds going to the library; or a visit to a farm. We encourage parents to go with us whenever possible. We plan parent meetings twice a year, parent conferences once a year, and our annual Family Picnic is usually in early June. We observe six of the major holidays.

Our address is
_____
_____

and our telephone number is _____ - _____ . If you have any questions, please feel free to call, or we would be happy for you to drop by for a visit and let us give you a tour of our facility.

Some Information

For Parents

About Our Program

Activities Include:

Outdoor Play

Creative Art

Self-selected Activities

Cooking Experiences

Woodworking

Water Play

Language Experiences

Field Trips

The World We Live In

Numbers And Counting

Music

Storytime

Our Community

Fingerplays

And Many More

Ruth Ann Ball,
Rose State College Child Development Center,
Midwest City OK

At _____

Children Learn To:

- work alone and with others
- share and take turns
- explore and expand abilities and interests
- express thoughts and ideas
- listen to others
- develop feelings of security and success

Nursery School Activities:

- science
- creative art
- housekeeping
- books
- music, listening
- block corner
- large muscle activities
- manipulative area
- rice table

Activities Are Designed To:

- build self-confidence
- develop vocabulary
- encourage recognition of differences in sound, size, shape and color
- increase interest in books, numbers and people
- improve coordination
- introduce new ideas

Daily Activities Schedule:

- arrival
- circle-theme of the week
- free play
- creative art
- learning tables: language arts, math, science, social studies
- quiet time/rest room
- fingerplays
- snack
- music and games
- story
- departure

To Enroll Your Child:

Call _____ to be placed on a waiting list.

Classes begin in September.

Children are placed on a first-come, first-served basis. Enrollment forms will be mailed to parents.

A physical exam is required for all children.

Cost:

Registration fee of $_____ and a monthly $_____ fee, prorated for the year

Carlene Thompson, Delaware JVSD, Delaware, OH

School Name

Phone Number

[School name
goes here
Address
City State ZIP]

At our school we believe every child is special and every child is unique.

Chapter Four

Parents and Teachers Working Together

Welcome!

During the first few weeks of school, don't be disturbed if your child:

- is shy and clings to you,
- is aggressive and won't share,
- hits and refuses to take turns,
- tires easily and cries a great deal,
- resists using the school bathroom, has accidents,
- doesn't talk much about what happened at school.

These are all symptoms of tension and stress in a new situation, and will disappear as your child becomes used to the teachers, other children and the classroom routines. Be sympathetic and supportive!

You can help by:

- letting the child bring in a favorite security-object (doll, blanket, etc.)
- letting the child just stand and watch, knowing observation is one way of participating
- not putting pressure on the child to produce something to take home
- not pushing the child to conform to routines without time to adjust
- allowing lots of time for personal routine, a nourishing breakfast and a pleasant, safe ride to school
- having a cheerful, *positive* attitude as the child leaves you, either at home or at school, such as: "Goodbye, I'll see you later!"
- encouraging talk about school by asking specific questions, such as: "Did you play with the _____ today?" or, "What was for snack today?" rather than "What did you do today?"

Remember always: the more relaxed the parent, the more relaxed the child.

Morning classes meet from _____ a.m. until _____ a.m.

Afternoon classes meet from _____ p.m. until _____ p.m.

(Late pick-ups from morning classes, and early arrivals for afternoon classes leave teachers without adequate preparation and lunch time. Please, be considerate and time your arrivals and dismissals properly.)

Helping Parent Days

As each of you comes in for an assigned helping day, you may experiences some — or all — of the following reactions:

- I want to dig a hole and crawl in, I'm so embarrassed!
- My child really *is not* this weird — I promise!

- Does my child *always* act this way?
- You must think I'm a *terrible* parent.

RELAX! Especially on your first day! But throughout the year, to varying degrees, your child may not be "with it" on your helping days. Crying, clinging, whining and anger are not unusual as your child learns to share you with friends and teachers. Or your child may ignore you; refuse to participate fully, sing or recite as you watch; or forget the routine. Teachers know that they need to relax and forgive. We urge you to do so with us.

Rather than talk about this situation in front of your child — which will make him/her even more self-conscious — give the teacher a call at home in the evening, or set up a conference before or after school on another day. Remember — a cooperative is a place for parents, teachers *and* children to learn together.

Children's Books About Starting School

Picture books about the beginning of school can help to lessen apprehensions, and most importantly, can open a channel of communication about school between you and your child — the start of a life-long habit. Using children's books to show that it can indeed help in times of stress. Story characters who model successful adjustments are an excellent resource for children as well as parents. The following books will reinforce positive feelings about school, and are appropriate *long* past the first day of school, as children work through first-time experiences and feelings:

- *It's Fun To Go To School.* by Joan Mellings (Hardcover/Harper and Row)
- *My Nursery School*, by Harlow Rockwell (Hardcover/Greenwillow; paperback/Picture Puffin).
- *Will I Have A Friend?* by Miriam Cohen (Hardcover/Macmillan; paperback/Colliers).
- *The First Day of School*, by Patricia Relf (A Golden Book).
- *Peter Goes To School*, by Wanda Rogers House (Wonder Books —Price/Stern/Sloan).
- *Betsy's First Day at Nursery School* by Gunilla Wolde (Random House).
- *Playbook* by Gwenda Turner (Hardcover/Viking Kestrel; paperback/Puffin Books).
- *You Go Away*, by Dorothy Corey (Hardcover/Albert Whitman).
- *Starting School*, by Janet and Allan Ahlberg (Hardcover/Viking)

For adults only: *How To Help Your Child Start School*, A Practical guide for Parents and Teachers Of Four to Six Year Olds, by Bernard Ryan, Jr. Perigee Books, G.P. Putnam's Sons.

Happy reading!

Cathy Griffin, Dutch Neck Presbyterian Cooperative Nursery School, Princeton Junction NJ

Personal Profile Sheet

Please complete this survey of your child and his/her interests. It will help me to become better acquainted with your child and better able to meet his/her needs.

Full Name

_____

First   Middle   Last

Nickname_____

Address_____

Telephone_____

Birthdate_____

Allergies_____

Favorite things:

_____

_____

_____

_____

Least favorite things:

_____

_____

Things you would like to see your child do in kindergarten:

_____

_____

Donna Henry, Portsmouth Catholic Elementary School, Portsmouth VA

Welcome Letter To Child

Dear _____,

It's almost time to start kindergarten! My name is _____, and I will be your teacher. We'll be having lots of fun playing and working together at school. I'm looking forward to meeting you on _____ when you come to visit with your mom or dad.

When we start school the next week, there'll be lots of time to play, read books, make things and learn. We'll spend a lot of time getting to know each other and making new friends, finding out how we are alike and how we are different.

I've been busy getting our classroom ready, and the real fun will start when all the kids are here!

I am looking forward to meeting you,

Constance Wilson, Union Memorial School, Colchester, VT

Walk In My Footsteps

Dear Parents:

You are invited to a special night at _____. The preschoolers would like you to see what it would be like to be their age again. They invite you to "walk in my footsteps" for an evening. There will be various activities available, such as fingerpaints, sand play, playdough, block building, etc.

Your preschooler can lead you by the hand through these learning avenues since they have become quite proficient at them through the years. Participation is necessary and quite fun. We will also join together before the evening is over to sing some songs. So, please keep _____, 19__ at _____ p.m. open. We hope to see everyone there.

Mona Vieu, St. Andrew's Preschool, St. Paul MN

Notebook Letter

Dear Parents,

Welcome to the 19___-___ school year. I am looking forward to an exciting and educational experience for your child. Please be prepared for days when your child returns home somewhat less clean than he/she arrived. I firmly believe children learn through exploration of their environment. The children will often be playing with materials such as paint, sand, pudding and water. For this reason, I am asking that you please send in an extra set of clothes for your child.

Since the children are brought to school by bus, limiting my time to keep you informed about your child's development, I am requesting that you provide your child with a notebook which will be used as a daily source of communication with you regarding your child and the class program. Feel free to write back to me in the notebook with any concerns, questions or comments you may have.

I am looking forward to working with your child. Your cooperation during this year will be greatly appreciated.

Regina Swierc, United Cerebral Palsy League of Union County, Union, NJ

End Of Year Thank You

Dear Parents,

Thank you for a wonderful year! We appreciate the support and cooperation you have given us throughout this school year. It has made our job a lot easier, and it has been a joy for us to have had the opportunity of getting to know you and your children.

It has been our privilege to be your children's teachers and to see these little ones grow and develop and gain confidence in themselves and their abilities. Thank you for allowing us to experience these precious moments with your children.

May your summer be wonderfully fun and relaxing, and may you and your families continue to grow in love together.

Sincerely,

Penny Hansen, Yorba Linda Methodist Nursery School, Yorba Linda CA

Me Museum

Dear Family:

We are glad to have your child in school. It has been fun getting to know each other.

We have been learning about each other, and as part of this activity we have set up a "Me Museum." Your child may bring in something he/she wants to "share" with all of us in the room (e.g., stuffed animal, picture, book, favorite toy, etc.) for their part of the "Me Museum."

Please put the items in a bag and label with your child's name. Your child will be spotlighted on

_____.

Thank you for your cooperation.

Barbara Smolens, Hempstead Public Schools, Pre-Kindergarten, Hempstead, NY

Putting Toys Away

Dear Parents,

Part of our philosophy at _____is to help children be responsible for themselves, their behavior and their property. The learning process for teaching "responsibility" seems never-ending at times.

We would like to have your help. When you pick up your child, allow them time to put away the toys or materials they are working with. This will help your child to learn that returning things to their appropriate place is important. Of course, if they are playing with the same manipulative as OTHER children, they only need to be encouraged to put away what they are using.

Thank you for being patient while we learn.

Sincerely,

Ruth Ann Ball, Rose State College Child Development Center, Midwest City OK

Topics Of Interest To Parents

Dear Parents:

As we discussed during our Parent Orientation, we are interested in developing a parent group, with meetings on varied topics. However, before we can make plans we need to know more about your interests and concerns. Your answers to the questions below will help us to assess your needs and interests.

Please check beside each topic to indicate your interest.

_____ Moral development of a young child

_____ Physical development of a young child

_____ Emotional/social development of a young child

_____ Practical life experiences at home

_____ Intellectual development of a young child

_____ Building self-esteem

_____ Management skills with young child

_____ Selecting books for the young child

_____ Music and the young child

_____ Sibling rivalry

_____ The effect of television on children

_____ Planning nutritional snacks

_____ The value of play

_____ Making learning activities for children

Some other interests that I would like covered in parent meetings: _____

The best day to attend a meeting is: (Circle your choice) M   T   W   T   F   S

I would like to meet: Every week _____, Every 2 weeks _____, once a month _____

The most convenient time for me to attend a meeting would be:_____

Please return this form to me. Thanks.

Lisa Gardner Warner, Eastern Kentucky University, Child Development Center, Richmond KY

Bringing Toys To School

Dear Parents,

It has come to our attention that there have been some problems with the children bringing toys to the Center. Some of these problems are:

1. The toys get broken and the children get upset;

2. The children give the toys away without permission from parents;

3. The children argue over the toys and their ownership.

To alleviate this problem, we are establishing a general one day show-and-tell each week. This will be Wednesday. On the other days, please have your children keep their toys and possessions at home. If the school-age children bring toys for school, they will have to put them away when they are the Center (except for Wednesdays). We could use your help in making the children understand our new rule.

In addition, the following items will be greatly appreciated for our arts and crafts projects:

- boxes
- cardboard milk containers
- juice cans
- magazines and newspapers
- buttons
- cloth scraps

Thank you so much for your help in the above matters,

Pam Humphrey, Takoma Park Day Care Center, Takoma Park MD

Bringing A Painting Home

Dear Parents,

Today your child is bringing home a painting! On days like this, you may find yourself thinking, "Good grief! *What is this?"*

Remember...art work is an expression of language. Many times a child won't be able to verbalize what it is that he/she has painted. Please observe how your child's art work develops as the school year progresses.

Many children will paint one color over another. This is the child's way of exploring the media. Also, some will start out with a specific idea in mind, and then gradually cover every figure on his/her paper. In other words, some of these paintings have a completely different painting *underneath*.

Please enjoy your child's art as his/her own self-expression. Give him/her a place to display this work, preferably at his/her eye level. Help your child develop an appreciation of self and the unique quality of his/her own art work by appreciating and enjoying your child.

Sincerely,

Maryann Poulton, Burbank Elementary School, Hayward CA

Don't Worry, Be Specific

Are you tired of asking your child, "What did you do in school today?" only to hear, "Nothing," "I don't know" or "I played."? If so, here's good news — help is available.

Something is wrong somewhere. It can't be the teacher — whoever heard of any teacher anywhere that lets children play in school ALL day! Nor is it likely that the problem is your child. So, what IS the problem? Why don't the children *tell* us what they did in school?

The trouble is the question! We're asking the *wrong* one! Try asking other questions and see if you get better answers. Many times, children have difficulty remembering because its hard to start at the beginning. When they get home, their day becomes history. It's over and they go onto the next thing in their lives. However there are a few pointers to keep in mind when questioning your child about school:

Avoid general questions like, "What did you do in school?"

Avoid questions that can be answered with a simple "yes" or "no," e.g., "Did your teacher like your Show and Tell rock?" or "How was school?" or "Any homework?"

Instead get specific. Say,

- "Who did you play with today?"
- "What was at the art center?"
- "Tell about the shape you're learning this week."
- "What do you know about fall?"
- "What choices did you make at playtime today?"
- "What did you do on Apple Day?"
- "Tell me about the Wildlife Preserve."
- "What jobs do Junior Nature Cadets have?"
- "What does 'Special Helper/Child of the Day/Line Leader' mean?"
- "What do you like most about school?" "Why?"
- "Did you play house today? Who were you? The Mom? The Baby? The Babysitter?"

These types of questions should get better answers which could even lead you and your child into some interesting and informative conversations. Best wishes as you begin building your bridge over the Communication Generation Gap!

Kathy Kalmar, Bloom Developmental Academy, Roseville MI

Communicating With Children

The most readily available tool parents and teachers have for dealing with children is the ability to communicate with the spoken word.

Good communication helps children develop confidence, feelings of self-worth and good relationships with others. It makes life with them more pleasant now and helps them grow into adults who have good feelings about themselves and others.

Talking with children involves the exchange of words, ideas and feelings between two people. Communication is what we say and how we say it. We communicate with looks (scowls and smiles), with actions (slaps and hugs), with silence (warm and cold) as well with words (kind and unkind).

How can we be successful in communicating with children?

1. Pay attention to what the child is saying — if you are busy, tell the child, "I'm busy, but let's talk about it later." Be sure to follow through.

2. Use "you-messages" to describe the child's feeling and encourage him/her to express his/her troublesome feelings. "You are upset because you didn't win the game."

3. Use "I" messages to express to the child how his/her actions make you feel. "I need help in picking up now", instead of "You sure made a mess." This gives the child responsibility for changing his/her own behavior.

4. Tell the child what to do rather than what not to do. "Hold your coat up so it won't drag on the ground." instead of "Don't drag your coat on the ground."

5. Make your request simple — young children have a hard time remembering several orders at a time.

6. Get the child's attention before speaking to him/her — "Erin, (wait until she looks at you) it is time to put the book away."

7. Make important requests firmly — give a reason why he/she must do this thing at this particular time.

8. Communicate at eye-level.

9. Try not to interrupt and scold children when they are telling you their stories.

10. Avoid unkind words which tear a child down such as:

- ridiculing — "You're acting like a big baby."
- shaming — "I'm ashamed of you."
- name-calling — "You're a bad girl."
- teasing
- threatening — "I'm going to tell your daddy if you don't stop doing that."
- Unkind words discourage the child and give him/her a poor concept of him/herself.

11. Use kind words to encourage and build up the child. "I liked the way you hung up your coat."

12. Instead of calling across the room, walk over to the child and speak calmly.

13. Forcing children to "mouth" the words, "I'm sorry," will not teach them to be sorry. It will teach them that they had better do as they are told, or they will be punished.

14. Speak in a quiet voice.

Expectations need to be communicated to children in a straightforward way. Parents and teachers facilitate the development of self-control in children by using positive guidance techniques and treating them with respect.

1. Set clear, consistent, fair limits for behavior.

2. Value mistakes as learning opportunities.

3. Redirect children to more acceptable activities.

4. Model and encourage expected behavior — we need to teach by example — act in ways you want your children to act.

5. Listen when children talk about their feelings and frustrations.

6. Guide children to resolve conflicts.

7. Patiently remind children of rules and why they are needed.

8. Be fair in your discipline — listen to the children.

Joyce Stockdill, Silver Spring Child Care Center, Silver Spring MD

Stages Of Art

Dear Parents,

Every now and then we become involved with a teaching principle that we feel you would find as fascinating as we do. One of those moments is taking place in our classroom right now; we'd like to share it with you. It has to do with the developmental stages that children pass through in their drawings.

There are basically five of these stages that can take place between the ages of two and six. By observing, we...and you, can learn a lot about how your child is maturing. Let's get into the stages so that you can understand the process.

Stage One: Random Scribbling...The very young child makes large arcs on the paper. They have no "visual" control over where the marks go. Here, however, the motor activity of using the entire arm is very important to their development.

Stage Two: Controlled Scribbling...Now, there is a greater variety of scribbles. The arcs get smaller because the child is using the wrist. Now, there is visual control. The child looks at the drawing until it is finished.

Stage Three: Names Scribbling...There is no doubt in the child's mind about what his or her picture is. Adults, however, can't recognize it. Drawings are *symbols* of the objects, events or experiences that the child has had. This is an important step because the child is using *abstract thought*. The child can see the relationship between the marks on the paper and the symbol or object.

Stage Four: Early Presentation...The drawings start to look like the objects they represent. There will be distortions in size. Usually, the most important part of the drawing will be much larger than the rest. *There drawings are still not adult pleasers*, but they are very important to the child. Also, by this time, the child has naturally changed the grip on the drawing instrument to an almost adult grip. Objects that are important to the child will appear.

Stage Five: Preschematic...The progression goes on very naturally. Now, objects are more relative to size. There is a right side up to the paper and a base line develops, i.e., green for grass, blue for sky. By this time, the child is using the wrist and fingers and has mastered an adult grip on the drawing instrument. Authorities have observed that when a child is doing closed forms in his or her drawings, the child will also be able to use closed forms in writing his or her name. If the child is in the early scribbling stages, the name will also be scribbled. If this is the case, the child should not be *forced* to print letters because he or she is not ready.

We find that the best thing that we, as adults, can do is to maintain an open attitude that is free of judgment. As soon as your child begins to identify symbols on the paper, he or she has no doubt as to what the drawing is. Therefore, he or she expects everyone else to know what it is. If your child proudly shows us a drawing, and we can't recognize it, we will usually say something like, "Tell me about it." Perhaps we'll pick out a part of the drawing and comment on it, i.e., "My, you have a lot of wiggly black lines there." This encourages your child to tell us about the drawing, and we haven't hurt any feelings by asking, "What is is?" According to authorities in this field, this question can be detrimental.

Actually, our job, as teachers and parents, is easy! Let it develop naturally. Don't force, show how or judge. Make plenty of blank paper and drawing instruments available to the children. Keep in mind that the *process* is more important than the *product*.

We hope that this information is helpful. We wanted to share it with you to help you to contunue being the most important people in your child's world.

Janice Freeman, The Growing Place Pre-School, Westlake Village CA

Feedback From Parents

We would like you to share how you feel your child is doing. No one knows your child as well as you do. Please take a moment and fill in this page and return it to us by _____, 19__. Add anything you feel would be helpful.

* **Where do you feel your child's strengths are? (circle all that apply)**

    social skills (playing with children, acting appropriately with adults, getting along with others)

    fine motor skills (dressing, cutting, drawing, printing)

    gross motor skills (climbing, running, balancing)

    speech and language (understand what is being said, being understood)

    readiness skills (naming/using colors, shapes, numbers, letters, attention span)

* **Where do you feel that your child's weaknesses are? (circle all that apply)**

    social skills

    fine motor skills

    gross motor skills

    speech and language

    readiness skills

* **Do you feel your child has made a good adjustment to school this year?**

* **List any questions you have that you feel we can help you with.**

Sandra DeVellis and Helen Murgida, The Pentucket Workshop, Inc., Georgetown MA

Potty Training Cooperation

Potty training can be easily accomplished, but it takes a lot of cooperation between parent and teacher. It is essential to be consistent with your child at home and the day care or it only confuses the child. Pants should be worn from the time your child wakes up in the morning until they go to bed. Remember, being consistent is the key to successful potty training. Wearing diapers during waking hours confuses children.

Clothes should be ones that are easily taken on and off, no one piece suits or suspender type clothing. Five to six pairs of training pants, extra clothing and a plastic bag should be brought to the daycare.

Don't make the child sit on the potty for long periods of time. Five minutes is long enough. The best times are as soon as they wake up, 20 to 30 minutes after a drink, after meals and before going to bed.

Always praise them when the potty is used.

GOOD LUCK!

Wendy Travis, ABC Daycare and Learning Center, North Charleston, SC

Dressed For Messy Play

Dear Mom and Dad,

Please send me to school dressed in clothing that I can get messy.

I promise to wear a smock when I am working with paint, clay, glue or anything messy, but accidents do happen.

Thank you for understanding. I love you.

Love,

Julia M. Rachinsky-Wood, Brookdale Nursery School, Inc., Stamford CT

The Caregiver And The Parent

Dear Parents,

Recently I was asked a question that prompted me to do some thinking. The question was: After spending so much time, energy and love with the children, does it bother me or hurt my feelings when Mom and/or Dad comes in and baby "goes crazy" with joy? That brings to mind three points:

1. I never realized that some parents may be concerned about this. Thank you but no, I'm not hurt — this is the way it should be. I am not a surrogate mother, nor am I meant to be. I am the Caregiver. I am interested with baby's care. I take this trust very seriously and consider it a privilege — but I am still a Caregiver.

2. Some parents may not have been able to observe this reaction in their child. They may feel uncomfortable with the relationship the child and I have developed. The relationship is during the hours the children are here and is important to the child's ability to cope and have successful experiences. But it takes nothing away from the child's relationship with Mom or Dad.

3. Sometimes a child acts as if he or she doesn't want to go home. There are several reasons for this. One, the child may have just started some new game or project and doesn't want to leave it. Two, he or she may be tired. They want to go home, but don't want to go through all the fuss and bother to get there. They do not prefer the teacher to parents, nor the school to home.

If parents have any concerns PLEASE feel free to speak to me (or your child's teacher). You ARE NOT the first to experience certain feelings concerning your child.

Peggy Dvorak, Old Lyme Daycare, Old Lyme CT

Parent Play Day

Once a year, each parent schedules a whole day to share his/her child's world and enjoy the all-too-brief preschool experience at _____.

If you are interested, you could share a project or concept (we'll help), "join the staff" or simply be a buddy to your child. We'll be sending the year's curriculum schedule home soon so you can pick a theme or focus you like. Plan your day as far in advance as possible to have the day all to *yourself*. Or be spontaneous as time opens up. But *plan* it, so we don't have to schedule several parents the last month of the year, please. In addition to *thrilling* your child, you will gain new insight into your child's reality. Plus, you will understand what it takes to keep twelve lively children happy and challenged (yet clean and calm) ten hours a day.

Please sign and return by _____, 19__. Thanks very much.

_____

Your child's name _____

Schedule my parent play day for:

Mother:

_____   _____
Best date   Name

Father:

_____   _____
Best date   Name

Melody Cornell, Hunter's House Preschool and Extended Daycare, Oakland CA

Parent-teacher Conference Letter

Dear Parents,

      As the day of our scheduled parent-teacher conference draws near, we need to collect our thoughts about your child so that our time can be put to good use. The following questionnaire is designed to assist me in covering all areas of concern to you and to me. Please, take a few minutes to complete and return it to me *prior to* our conference. Remember, this is *not* an evaluation, it is a *sharing* of information about a child that we both care about. Thank you for your cooperation.

1. My child communicates the following to me at home about school:

      a. relationships with children and adults

      b. favorite activities and areas of play

2. I see my child's areas of strength as:

3. I feel that my child needs to develop skills in:

4. I would like to discuss or have more information on:

Have you considered the whole child — social, emotional, physical and intellectual?

Cathy Griffin, Dutch Neck Presbyterian Cooperative Nursery School, Princeton Junction NJ

Pre-conference Form

Dear Parents of _____,

　　　If you desire, please sign up for a parent/teacher conference time on the easel near the front door of the nursery school. In order for the teacher to plan for this conference, it is important that you express your feelings, interests and areas of concern.

　　　Please respond to the following items and return a copy to the teacher as soon as possible (and no later that one full week before your conference). Your help will be appreciated.

What is your child's attitude toward school?

What are his/her out of school interests and activities?

Is there anything else you might tell us about your child which will help us to know him/her better?

Suggested topics for the conference:

follows directions　　　　　　　　health　　　friends　　　math readiness

gets along well with others (students and teachers)　　　art　　　　respect for authority

music　　　　　　　　　　respect for other people's property　　　dance/movement

self-confidence　　　　　　reading readiness　　　self-control　science work habits

working with a group　　　　listening/paying attention　other_____

From the above areas, select three that you would like to discuss during the conference and list them below.

　　　1._____

　　　2._____

　　　3._____

Yvonne D. Langley, Sleepy Hollow Nursery School, Scarborough NY

Scheduling Parent-teacher Conference

Dear_____,

    As you know, parent-teacher conferences are used to discuss your child's progress.

    I hope you will be able to come to school on _____,
_____,19___ at _____ so we can talk together about
_____.

    Feel free to jot down questions that might come to mind about school. This will be a time to consider these.

    We realize how difficult it is for most fathers to participate in afternoon conferences, but you are asked to come if it is possible.

Sincerely,

_____

Please return this confirmation to school as soon as possible.

I/We will be able to attend a conference on:

_____, _____, 19___ at _____.

This time is not convenient. I would like to suggest the following time: _____,
_____, 19___ at _____.

_____
Signature

Charlotte Swanson, Century Oaks School, Elgin IL

A Survey For All Parents And Guardians

1) On a scale of 1 (poor) to 10 (excellent) how would you rate the following?

        a) our program in general _____
        b) teachers _____
        c) physical facilities _____
        d) supplies & equipment ____
        e) food _____
        f) field trips _____
        g) administration
        h) other _____

2) In order to keep up with inflation and growing costs should the Center (yes or no)

    cut field trips? _____
    reduce staff? _____
    other _____
    increase tuition? _____
    have a sliding scale tuition? _____
    have a parent-led fund-raiser? _____
    have a summer field trip fee? _____

3) What other suggestions do you have for generating more funds and/or reducing costs?

_____

_____

_____

5) Would you be willing to take an active role in fund-raising?

        yes_____
        no_____

6) Would you be available to serve as a parent representative on the Day Care Board?

        yes_____
        no_____

Please return this survey to the Day Care Center by _____, _____.

Pam Humphrey, Takoma Park Day Care Center, Takoma Park MD

Annual Survey

Dear Parents:

We appreciate your ideas and look forward to your comments in our annual survey. Please answer the following questions in the space provided (use the reverse side if you need more space).

1. How did you find _____?

2. Can you recommend for or against other schools you encountered in your research? We like to visit and network with other schools as appropriate.

3. What specifically made you pick *this* school?

4. Is there anything that distinguishes this school from others with which you are familiar?

5. Have you seen or heard of anything at another school that you'd like to see here? Please give details.

6. What would you like to see *never* changed?

7. What would you like to see changed? How? Why?

8. Do you plan to keep your child at _____ until kindergarten?

9. Do you foresee any upcoming scheduling changes?

    We'd appreciate your thoughts on any of the following items. Please add anything else you'd like to discuss.

> the physical space and learning centers
>
> outside play space
>
> school animals
>
> routines, e.g., toothbrushing and handwashing; placemat clearing
>
> staff quality and quantity and availability
>
> parent conferences
>
> festivities and extended family get-togethers
>
> changing themes and special programs
>
> field trips
>
> meals and cooking class
>
> photographs
>
> variety and quality of learning experiences
>
> quality of care
>
> dynamics between children and staff
>
> special support through parent meeting

    Thank you so much for your investment of time and thought in your school. This survey is very valuable to us — your detailed responses and evaluation keep us one of the best schools we have found. As you know by now — when you talk, we listen! We care more and it shows.

    Please return this form by _____. Again, thank you.

Melody Cornell, Hunter's House Preschool and Extended Day Care, Oakland CA

Responsibilities Of Parents In The Co-op

1. Participation in the administration of the School, individually and through the Executive Committee.

2. Attendance at all General Membership meetings; usually three per year. This does not mean signing in and leaving!

3. Fulfillment of helping parent responsibilities. (Failure to fulfill obligations — $_____ fine.) Starting time for helping parents is _____. Tardiness can result in a fine as this is a most important time to teachers and parents for establishing the day's schedule. A parent is expected to fulfill all helping parent responsibilities. In the event of extenuating circumstances, prior approval, including the signing of the State Disclosure forms, is required. (State Disclosure forms may be obtained from the Vice President.)

4. Fulfillment of housekeeping duties, usually one per year per child enrolled, which involves dusting, vacuuming, washing tables in classrooms, cleaning workrooms and cleaning paint from bathrooms. (Failure to fulfill obligations — $_____ fine.)

5. Completion and return of all forms on time.

6. Keeping school records up-to-date — including changes in address, phone number, health status, emergency numbers.

7. Prompt payment of tuition and other obligations.

8. Active service on one committee. (Failure to fulfill obligation $_____ fine.) Committee participation is a major portion of your co-op responsibility.

9. Participation in all fund-raising activities. The _____ school, being a non-profit organization, cannot accumulate profits. Therefore, we must raise new funds each school year to provide an exceptional facility. Each year our fund-raisers enable us to renew as well as replenish our school.

In order to continue to provide sturdy, abundant and creative tools for enjoyable learning, it is most important that every member currently enrolled supports all of our fund-raising projects. Your support of our fund-raising committee keeps our tuition competitive with other schools and establishes our cooperative atmosphere in which we all take pride.

Fund-raising projects occur throughout the year. The number of fund-raising projects is determined by the fund-raising committee. Major projects require mandatory participation by all members. A $_____ penalty will be imposed for each of the major projects in which *no* participation is recorded.

10. All members of _____ are expected to adhere to the rules and regulations of the organization. Failure to do so may result in fines being levied or in dismissal from the organization by the Board of Directors.

11. Upon your failure to fulfill three of the above-stated obligations, your child will be dismissed from _____. Please note that payment of fines for failure to fulfill these obligations, though required, does not remove the failed obligation from your record.

12. All offenses will carry over for the duration of the family's membership in the co-op.

These rules are not intended to be punitive. Our intent is to make our school a happy cooperative so that everyone may continue to enjoy our program and facilities.

Cathy Griffin, Dutch Neck Presbyterian Cooperative Nursery School, Princeton Junction NJ

Chapter 5

Love
and
Discipline

Teach Him Gently...If You Can...

My young son starts to school tomorrow...It's all going to be strange and new to him for a while, and I wish you would sort of treat him gently...

You see, up to now, he's been our little boy.

He's been boss of the backyard...His mother has always been around to repair his wounds, and I've always been handy to soothe his feelings.

But now, things are going to be different...

This morning he's going to walk down the front steps, wave his hand, and start out on the great adventure...It's an adventure that will probably include wars and tragedy and sorrow.

To live his life in the world he will live in requires faith and love and courage.

So, world, I wish you would sort of take him by his young hand and teach him the things he will have to know.

Teach him, but gently...if you can.

He will have to learn, I know, that all are not just, that all are not true.

But teach him also that for every scoundrel there is a hero...that for every selfish politician, there is a dedicated leader...Teach him that for every enemy, there is a friend.

It will take time, world, I know, but teach him, if you can, that a nickel earned is of far more value than a dollar found...Teach him to lose...and to enjoy winning.

Steer him away from envy, if you can, and teach him the secret of quiet laughter.

Let him learn early that bullies are the easiest people to lick...Teach him, if you can, the wonder of books...But also give him quiet time to ponder the eternal mystery of birds in the sky, bees in the sun, and flowers on a green hillside.

In school, world, teach him it is far more honorable to fail than to cheat...Teach him to have faith in his own ideas, even if everyone tells him they are wrong...Teach him to be gentle with gentle people and tough with tough people.

Try to give my son the strength not to follow the crowd when everyone else is getting on the bandwagon...Teach him to listen to all men...But teach him also to filter all he hears on a screen of truth and take only the good that comes through.

Teach him, if you can, how to laugh when he is sad...Teach him there is no shame in tears...Teach him there can be glory in failure and despair in success.

Teach him to scoff at cynics and to beware of too much sweetness...Teach him to sell his brawn and brains to the highest bidder but never to put a price tag on his heart and soul.

Teach him to close his ears to a howling mob...and to stand and fight if he thinks he's right.

Treat him gently, world, but don't coddle him, because only the test of fire makes fine steel.

Let him have courage to be impatient...let him have the patience to be brave.

Teach him always to have sublime faith in himself...Because then he will always have sublime faith in mankind.

This is a big order, world, but you see what you can do...He's such a fine little fellow, my son!

Sheila M. Cole, G.C.C.C. Campus Child Care Center, Garden City KS

Bonding

Dear Parents,

I would like to share one of my philosophies with you. You do not have to agree with them; but if they make you think and form your own opinion, they have done their job.

Bonding is a term that refers to forming a relationship of trust. Parents usually bond with their children at birth. It is an intensely powerful bond and the major one for a child in his/her early years. Slowly the child forms other bonds — with grandparents, babysitters, close friends. Soon your child will be forming his/her first bond with a teacher at preschool. This bond is very important. Until a child feels safe and secure in the room and trust the adults in charge of his/her care, he/she cannot be free to learn and grow. My major goal in the first months is to make sure your child and I have bonded.

For some children it is easy. You may have seen some of the children on the first day hug and kiss me as if they have known me all their lives. That is their personality. Others keep a sharp eye on me and hope I will not come too near them. They want to watch and see. Some bond with me verbally.

Please watch and listen for signs that indicate how your child and I are doing in this area. Practice looking for non-verbal signs and spontaneous comments. A direct question — Do you like your teacher? — will confuse him/her.

Over the years I have realized that the bonds I form with parents relate to the bonds I form with the children. The more we work at developing a friendship and trust, the easier it is for your child to trust me and be free to learn and grow. This trust does not mean that you accept me unconditionally, but you feel that you can question me and that I will listen. Bonding for us starts with communication.

It is also important to close a bond when a relationship is over. I do this the last month of the school year when children are graduating to kindergarten. It is natural. They are excited about growing up and so am I. But sometimes a relationship ends sooner. If you know you are leaving before the end of the year, please let me know so your child and I can close our bond. I once had a child whose mother picked him up one day and said it was his last day. I went home and felt so angry. I didn't understand why because I could easily replace the child in the classroom and I understood the mother's circumstances. Then I realized I had spent two months bonding with him and in minutes he was gone. No goodbyes.

Other tidbits: I don't think a child will bond with a teacher if the child feels the parents do not like the teacher. The child knows how the parent feels. I have also read research that concluded that a child will learn equally well from a "good" teacher as from a "poor" teacher if he/she bonds and trusts the teacher. Interesting!

Linda Williams, The Punkin Seed Child Development Center, Lebanon OR

I Believe

Dear Parents,

As the new school year begins, the first thing I ask is that you to trust me with your children. I know it isn't easy. I do not want you to trust me only because of my education, experience or reputation. I want you to know my philosophy of teaching and children.

- I believe
- I believe children deserve respect.
- I believe that children should not be humiliated, hurt or embarrassed.
- I believe a child's self esteem should be treated with TLC.
- I believe a child has the right to go to the bathroom.
- I believe that children should be taught rather than trained.
- I believe my job is to teach until a child learns, rather than punish until he/she learns.

I want children to be good because it feel good and life is more enjoyable when we are not in conflict. I do not want children to be good for me, for my love, or because I am more powerful than they are.

I believe at any given point in time a person is doing the best he/she can with what he/she has. It is not always easy. I want your children to enjoy learning. They will if they are allowed to develop their own motivation. They will if they are successful in their attempts. They will if they enjoy the process of learning as well as the end product. They will if they learn according to their own inner timetable and their own style.

I believe we hurt a child's natural curiosity and motivation when we confuse them by adding rewards of love or artificial reinforcements. The response should not be "I am so proud of you." but rather, "You should be proud of yourself", Doesn't it feel good?" or "Isn't that exciting?"

I believe that in an open environment, such as preschool or home, there are always choices for a child. A child should be encouraged to be in charge of his/her learning. I believe modeling is, by far, the method that dominates a child's learning. I believe love makes a difference. As a teacher, it works far better than anger.

I believe we should protect our children as much as possible until we are sure they are strong. Then we can help them adjust to the realities of life. I do not believe children grow strong when they are asked to adjust to the realities of life as a form of education. In most situations we ask children to adjust because adults won't.

My job is not to control the children, but to help them control themselves.

I believe that if I am willing to say, "I am sorry," when I make a mistake, I do not have to be afraid of making a mistake.

Linda Williams, The Punkin Seed Child Development Center, Lebanon OR

Naughtiness

We raise our children either positively or negatively and somehow negatively has always been easier! "No" comes out of our mouths without thinking. "Yes" always takes thought! Negative techniques need to be balanced with positive ones. It is like walking a thin line or staying in the middle of the road. If we can identify the extremes in a situation, it is usually easier to stay in the middle.

Naughtiness is the biggest complaint of parents of preschoolers. The two extreme ways of dealing with it are:

1. Ignoring the behavior and thinking it will go away, and

2. Not allowing your child to have any negative feelings about themselves.

First, think about how much naughtiness is natural. Adults are naughty, too. We think bad thoughts, get angry at store clerks, get angry at ourselves, gossip, get angry at inanimate objects, like the car. But we are adults. We handle anger in socially acceptable ways. Children are still learning and it takes time. We need to categorize every "you can't" and give a "you can" choice each time. Over and over. It makes sense to us if we say, "Don't hit baby," we mean now and forever. To a child, we mean now. He/She did not know he/she had to remember the rule every day! His/Her idea of forever is limited!

Secondly, what are the appropriate and acceptable ways for your child to vent anger and frustration in your home?

After you answer that question, here are some guidelines:

1. Never ask a question when you already know the answer. "Did you take that rattle away from the baby?" He/She will tell you the answer he/she thinks you want to hear, which is usually a "lie," because he/she loves you and doesn't want to make you angry. Responding to a situation with, "Why did you do that again?" or "I am so sick of telling you over and over to stop it," makes a child feel "I am bad and I am stupid."

2. State the facts and state the consequences. "I see you did this. Go take a break in your room until I can cool off. I love you but I do not like what you did."

3. Find time, when the situation is over, to hug and talk about the problem and how you can both work to handle it better in the future. Explain how you feel. Express your confidence that he/she will learn other ways to behave.

4. Be ready to profusely apologize if you ever call it wrong! Parents aren't perfect. We jump to the wrong conclusions and yell first. (But if we can blow it, we have to allow the same right to our children. We all make mistakes so we need to forgive equally.)

Linda Williams, The Punkin Seed Child Development Center, Lebanon OR

A Child Develops With Love

Our first objective is to provide a climate for children to develop socially, emotionally, physically and intellectually. We are successful with this objective with the aid of you, the parent. As you strive to provide the very best for your child, may we offer a few suggestions that will help your child through his/her preschool years:

1. By your actions and words, assure your child that you love them.

2. Provide time to share activities with your children that are of interest to them.

3. Read to your preschooler.

4. Set a daily routine and stick to it as close as possible.

5. Make sure he/she gets plenty of rest (8-12 hours).

6. Be an example of what you want your child to be.

Your preschool child is a very important part of your life. He/She demands a lot of your time and talents, and returns all your efforts with one big hug and kiss. Appreciate your child and be assured that you are not alone as you strive to provide the very best for your child.

Sheila Cole, Garden City Community College, Campus Child Care Center, Garden City KS

What Do We Do?

Many parents have inquired about "what do we do" with a child whose behavior is out-of-control, aggressive or disruptive. It is now a requirement of our licensing that parents be notified in writing what our policy of discipline is and how it is implemented.

The staff shall not use abusive, neglectful, corporal, humiliating or frightening punishment under any circumstances. No child shall be physically restrained unless it is necessary to protect the safety and health of the child or others.

Removal of a child from the group for disciplinary or health reasons shall be to a location where visual supervision by staff shall be maintained.

What this means in practice is that reason and understanding underlie our dealings with children. Generally, a teacher will take a child aside and speak to him/her about the behavior. Children may be asked to choose a different activity for a while until materials can be used with more care. Children may be separated to reduce aggression.

A "time-out" may be an option, asking a child to sit in his/her cubby or on a chair briefly and observe. Sometimes the teacher must take a child out of the room. The teacher stays with the child, holding him/her kindly, firmly. At that time, the director or parent volunteer may step in to help with the balance of the group. Behavior which continues after these measures, has a high degree of intensity or causes injury to other children is cause for concern and intervention. A parent-teacher conference to discuss the behavior (actually "symptoms" of feelings) is the next step. And, in some cases, outside professional help is recommended.

Our staff is able by education and experience to identify behavior which is causing a child to be unhappy, participating at less than the usual level or stressed. These "symptoms" ask for patience, understanding and intervention which is not punishing. It is always imperative that home and school cooperate with mutual goals and procedures.

Thank you for your cooperation.

Carol D. McGee, Noroton Presbyterian Nursery School, Darien CT

Biting

Dear Parents,

"Bite" is a word that brings to mind all forms of fears and worries. We try to catch the deeds before they happen, but, unfortunately, it is not always possible. Children, especially toddlers, are not always very verbal, do not or cannot verbalize feelings and often show their feelings physically. As they grow older, with our help and guidance, they will learn to replace biting with appropriate responses.

There are no panaceas. If your child bites, all it means is that he or she has found this to be an effective response. Biting is usually provoked. Some children choose hitting, pushing or other responses. Some never do any of these. A lot of it comes down to personality, reinforcement, environment or chance.

This problem has never failed to come up in almost every class I've attended. We are not alone in trying to cope with this problem. Understanding and support for the other parents, children (and teachers) can only help. No one wants their child to bit or to be bitten. Or to hit or be hit. Or to be pushed, shoved or scratched. These are all normal children with normal problems, and the best we can do is to help one another while the children grow past these undesirable traits.

Donna Ruhland, Home Daycare, Dayton OH

Discipline Policy

We believe that children learn best through experiences. We believe that the teachers must lovingly guide and redirect the children to help them to learn to cooperate with their peers and to have positive, educational experiences to encourage and enhance their growth and development while in our care. We believe that we can best accomplish this by:

1. Having a variety of activities for the children.

2. By the use of group management techniques, limiting the number of children in each area of the room to avoid overcrowding and to allow for sufficient materials and the opportunity for constructive interactions.

3. By using a below the state recommended ratio of adults to student (the state requirement for three year olds is 1:10 we provide 1:7. The State requirement for four year olds is 1:15, we provide 1:9).

4. By speaking with a child if their behavior is inappropriate for the area or material that they are using, i.e., we take the blocks down; this is the way we use the paint brush; walking only please; etc.

5. By using positive language with the children to give praise for appropriate behavior, i.e., "I like the way John is sitting"; we say "only walking" instead of "don't run."

6. After using the above techniques, if a child is having a problem cooperating in an area of the room, he/she is asked to go to another area for awhile, i.e., "Peter, I'm sorry but that is not how we play in the sandbox, please go into the other room to the puzzle table or the house corner." As the year progresses, the children are just redirected to another area; they know that it means the behavior was not appropriate.

   • If group behavior is a problem, the area that has become a problem for the group to handle is closed and the group is broken up and redirected to other activities in the room.
   • If cleaning up is a problem for the entire group, we discuss it, and incorporate the "logical consequence" technique, which is, "if we take a long time to clean up, because the teachers have to remind, redirect and put the children back on task, then we run out of time for the fun things, like singing, story, outdoor play, etc..." This helps the children realize and internalize responsibility and what can happen.

7. Sometimes just a touch on the shoulder can let a child know of your presence and this will in turn put him/her back on task, such as attending to the lesson at circle time.

8. After exhausting these methods, if a child still has a problem with appropriate behaviors, the child is asked to sit on the thinking chair, which is a time out place to think about what he/she has done and with the help of teacher's discussions with him/her, what might be a

better way to interact with the other children, materials, etc. Thinking time lasts for five to ten minutes, approximately. Repeated trips to think in a given session would indicate to the teacher that a informal conference with the parent at dismissal time was in order, to inform the parent and to enlist their assistance in working with their child.

9. If a child is having consistent difficulties, or becomes distracting to the entire group (usually at circle time) he/she is asked to sit in the other room with a teacher so that he/she can think in a quieter atmosphere. He/She is still in sight of the Head Teacher and when there is a break in activities, the Head Teacher will speak with the child in a problem-solving manner.

10. Children with consistent difficulties are taken through the above procedures, and the parents are counseled regularly; if necessary, outside assistance is sought and, ultimately, the child could be dismissed from the program. This is seriously considered when the health, safety and welfare of this child, and/or that of another child or the children of the group are at risk.

11. Please be advised that under the law any form of hitting, corporal punishment, abusive langauge, ridicule, harsh or humiliating or frightening treatment, is illegal and is against our philosophy. NONE of these behaviors will ever take place at _____.

12. On a final note, we try to be as consistent as possible with our classroom rules so that the children will know what is expected of them. We find that this helps the children and leads to their success.

Margaret Gibson-Adams, The Presbyterian Nursery School on the Green, Bloomfield NJ

Chapter 6

Play
and
Learning

Gee, All Those Kids Seem To Do Is Play

Yes, children here at _____ do play a lot. . . .75 to 90 minutes per session. During this time a lot is going on. They are:

- meeting friends
- playing with toys
- exploring how things work
- looking at books
- listening to music
- sharing
- pouring and measuring in the sand box
- having different experiences in a mostly child group situation vs. a mostly adult situation
- developing and expanding their language abilities
- having creative art experiences
- having cooperative play experiences
- learning to share the adults' attention
- learning social skills needed to play games and make friends
- building with materials that may not be available at home
- using "messy" art materials in a space provided for experimentation
- trying on different personalities with different clothing
- becoming independent
- comparing and contrasting different experiences
- learning from others while broadening their horizons

SO YOU SEE, WHAT LOOKS LIKE PLAY IS REALLY HARD WORK!

Margaret Gibson-Adams, The Presbyterian Nursery School on the Green, Bloomfield NJ

Our Philosophy Of Learning

In a caring and positive atmosphere, we create a warm and happy place for preschoolers to learn. As we bridge the gap from home to school, we guide children to a continued good self-image while building social skills in a school setting.

Sensory, motor, perceptual and language skills are introduced through materials and activities which are both child-centered and teacher-directed. Work is planned which emphasizes *the process rather than the product,* fostering a sense of accomplishment and pride.

Based on the theory that *children learn through play*, classroom routines encourage active involvement, meaningful experimentation and reinforcement through repetition. Schedules are designed which balance structure and free choice, as well as active and quiet times.

Recognizing that *children grow in predictable stages*, we treat each child as an individual, working from the level each child has attained and moving forward a step at a time. We teach *a love of learning* by allowing children to experience their own stage of development and helping them to feel *success without pressure.*

We value the active involvement of parents in our program, both through committee and classroom participation. Helping parent days enable the children to see their parents as important and concerned members of the new school environment, while providing parents with opportunities to view the child with teachers and other children.

Parents may gain valuable insights and techniques from the expertise of the staff; and, at the same time, share their own talents and interests to maintain the excellent quality here at _____. School then becomes a shared experience which hopefully will continue throughout each child's educational process.

Cathy Griffin, Dutch Neck Presbyterian Church Cooperative Nursery School, Princeton Junction NJ

Curriculum & Instruction

Our curriculum is developed through teacher observation and evaluation of each child. Concepts and skills are introduced which are appropriate to each child's stage of development, and which reinforce social, emotional, physical and intellectual growth. Concrete, hands-on activities and experiences are planned according to a calendar of themes and units which are relevant to the children, providing meaningful learning.

According to the Swiss psychologist Jean Piaget, who has exercised the greatest influence on early childhood education, children's learning occurs as a result of tactile experiences with objects in their environment. By manipulating objects and exploring on their own, they obtain information. As they relate new ideas to information they already know, more learning takes place. Children move beyond rote memory recall when adults provide them with concrete materials and guide them through their own first-hand discoveries. Sensory interaction is essential if children are to handle symbols well later on.

Erik Erickson explains the development of personality by the ways in which children interact with the environment and how they solve problems. The direction of growth is affected by the way that the environment supports the child and the way the child fulfills the standards of significant persons. A child feels a sense of accomplishment and belonging through successful child-initiated activity as well as adult-child interactions.

For over sixty years, the Gesell Institute for Human Development has studied the motor and social behavior of children through their language and adaptive skills. While the rate of growth is different for each child, it is highly patterned, predictable and cannot be rushed. Age norms are not to be used as standards or expectations, but as averages to assist in assessment of growth. Appropriate manipulative and symbolic play activities will support the stage the child has attained.

Academic workbooks and worksheets which demand visual, motor and cognitive ability beyond preschool development create emotional stress and a sense of failure for most children, and do not lead to significant strides in learning. The whole child goes to school, not just the brain. A child's intelligence needs to be supported by the rest of development, using the child's potential for school success. Rather than pushed or hurried from one stage to another, children need to be prepared by experience for each major change.

Cathy Griffin, Dutch Neck Presbyterian Church Cooperative Nursery School, Princeton Junction, NJ

From Us To You

We've been in school together for about two months and we wanted to give you some information about what your child does during the day. We hope you find this feedback helpful.

About me at _____

I enter into classroom activities:

At free play times, I usually spend my time in:

My favorite area of school is:

My favorite time of the school day is:

At circle time, I:

At group time, I:

I talk:

I can be understood:

I use my hands to:

When I use my body, the teachers notice:

One of the things I am learning to do is:

One of the things I do best is:

Sandra DeVellis and Helen Murgida, The Pentucket Workshop, Inc., Georgetown MA

Cover Letter For Progress Report

Dear Parents,

As the progress reports go home today I would like to send you a few words of explanation. Our progress report was designed to give you an indication of your child's growing readiness skills and maturity. During the preschool year, you child's adjustment to the group, the teachers, the other children and his or her fine and gross motor development, as well as the more "academic" aspects of readiness are all equally important factors to his or her success in school.

I am always concerned when putting progress reports in writing that parents or children will try to project the progress of a child's academic career. Remember, a four year old is an extremely changeable being. Growth and maturity occur at different stages and rates in each child. Sometimes this development occurs gradually, and sometimes in spurts, but as parents and educators, we can usually count on a year's growth in a year's time. This written report is meant to be a continuation of the ongoing communication we will have this year about your child. Please do not hestitate to drop me a note if you wish to discuss the report. I am available most afternoons for conferences.

Please do not sit down with your child and discuss the report item by item. Rather, look at the report as a whole and observe any patterns. Then sit down with your child and affirm his or her strengths. If you note a problem is in the control of the child (i.e., listening during group time), explain to him or her how to do better. Please do not chastise your child for things not in his or her control (adequate pencil grip). These items are included in the report card for your information about your child's development.

I also ask you not to make comparisons of your preschool child's report with that of your older child or of another preschooler. It is probably best not to discuss your preschooler's progress with your other children as they often do not understand what a small child can change and what he or she cannot change.

I have taken your time with this lengthy letter because I have seen so many parents and children hurt by unfavorable comparisons or negative feedback. I feel strongly that parents should have a detailed observation of their children's work, but children's emerging self-awareness and self-esteem need not be damaged if they are experiencing a difficulty of some sort.

Sincerely,

Mary Ann Bognar, St. Edward-Epiphany School, Richmond VA

Progress Report (1)

Your child _____ is showing progress in the following areas:

1. Intellectual Skills

    _____a. identifying shapes, sizes, numbers, alphabet and colors
    _____b. utilizing self-help skills
    _____c. investigating science activities
    _____d. engaging in early math concepts, counting, matching, addition and subtraction
    _____e. displays listening skills
    _____f. developing attention span
    _____g. exhibits decision making skills

2. Positive Self-image

    _____ a. recognizing self as an individual
    _____ b. displays feelings of acceptance and genuine liking of others
    _____ c. engages in successful activities

3. Relating To Others Individually And In A Group Situation

    _____ a. participates in sharing cooperation
    _____ b. identifies and expresses feelings
    _____ c. engages in group time/individual activities

4. Creativity And Imagination

    _____a. Explores art media
    _____b. Participates in dramatic play activities
    _____c. Uses resourcefulness during activities

5. Body Mastery

    _____a. participates in gross, fine and perceptual motor skills
    _____b. participates in designed running, hopping, jumping, skipping and walking activities
    _____c. pursues small muscle dexterity through designed activities and materials

Carlene Thompson. Delaware JVSD, Delaware OH

Progress Report (2)

Name _____ School _____

Evaluation Symbols

M = mastered
S = satisfactory
N = needs more time and assistance

Personal And Social Development

Knows Information Circled:

first name,   last name,   address,   phone number,   age

Takes Care Of Personal Needs As Circled:

uses utensils,   toileting,   brushes teeth,   handwashing,
puts belongings away,   assists in clean-up

_____works well with other
_____adjusts easily to new situations
_____shares and takes turns
_____follows routine and direction of teacher
_____initiates interaction with others
_____participates in group activities
_____plays independently
_____plays cooperatively with two to three children
_____plays cooperatively with four to five children
_____communicates through dramatic play
_____expresses ideas through various media

Cognitive Development

_____knows opposites
_____names body parts
_____counts one to five objects
_____counts five to ten objects
_____knows colors
_____knows shapes
_____sorts groups of objects
_____pairs objects
_____can sequence events/objects
_____copies a pattern of blocks
_____can draw a figure
_____recalls four items/events from a story
_____completes seven piece puzzle
_____completes ten piece puzzle

Motor Development

Gross Motor Skills

_____ hops
_____ jumps
_____ kicks a ball
_____ skips
_____ climbs
_____ catches a ball
_____ throws a ball
_____ balances
_____ pedals a bicycle

Fine Motor Skills

_____ traces, copies
_____ holds a pencil/crayon
_____ builds/constructs
_____ pastes/ glues
_____ controls, maniuplates
_____ prints own name

Dressing Skills

_____ puts coat/jacket on self
_____ snaps
_____ buttons
_____ zips
_____ uses *Velcro* fasteners
_____ ties
_____ laces shoes

Communications Development

_____ listens while others speak
_____ follows directions
_____ demonstrates concepts
_____ expresses ideas/feelings
_____ uses three to four word sentences
_____ recalls sequenced events
_____ recites fingerplays
_____ uses compound sentences
_____ uses six to eight word sentences

Teacher Comments:

Cheryl B. Lucas, Preschool Development Programs, Inc., Pittsburgh PA

What I Learned This Year

Dear Preschool Parent,

This preschool year has acted as a period of transition for your child from the narrow boundaries of his/her home and immediate family to the broader world of school and community. Throughout this academic year, your child has acquired the ability to work and play cooperatively; to follow instructions; to get along with other children; to respect and obey his/her teacher; and to adapt him/herself to separation from home to becoming happy in a new environment. Learning to adjust socially and emotionally is very necessary before a child is ready for more formal instruction.

Also, your child has been encouraged to become self-reliant in such basics as dressing and safety and health habits.

One of the basic indications of a child's readiness for kindergarten or first grade is his or her muscular coordination, particularly the coordination of eye and finger muscles. Many of the children have developed this through fingerplays, games, music, rhythms, art, and many other activities.

A recent study shows that children with some preschool educational experience (kindergarten or nursery school) showed higher I. Q. scores than those who did not attend. Research indicates that, in many cases, children with a high degree of motor development are more receptive to learning and tend to excel in their academic efforts.

We feel that each child has shown appreciable development during this year, and many are consequently prepared for kindergarten instruction.

It has been a pleasure working with you and your child.

Herman E. Walston, Kentucky State University, Rosenwald Early Childhood Learning Center, Frankfort KY

Chapter Seven

Birthdays
Holidays
and
Special Days

Halloween Events

Halloween, Halloween, Oh what funny things are seen.
Witches Hats, Coal Black Cats, Broom Stick Riders, Mice and Rats.

Day — Event #1

In observance of Halloween, the boys and girls will be performing tricks and receiving treats. The staff is always eager to see the children in their costumes and expressed a keen interest in presenting them with goodies. (Reminder: No masks or heavy make-up, please.)

Younger children will be trick o' treating between the hours of 9-11 a.m. and the afterschool children from 3-4 p.m. Infants and younger toddlers will not take part in this activity. However, special goodies will be provided for them in the Center.

Evening — Event #2

On _____ evening _____, from _____ to _____, the children and their parents (all dressed in costumes) are invited to a grand Halloween Carnival. The children's brothers and sisters, and parent's nieces and nephews under the age of 14 years, are also invited to attend this event. A Center parent and the entire staff have planned a variety of activities and games for children on that evening. A few games for parents, too. Approximately _____ children and their parents will be in attendance at this affair.

Some of the planned activities are: Halloween Pre-Show Musical, Pumpkin Pinata, Fishing Booth, Ghost Story Room, Fortune Teller, Spooky Room, Haunted House, Pumpkin Carving Ceremony, Monster Mash Dance Contest, Best Homemade Costume Contest, Bobbing for Apples, Balloon Chairs, Pin the Tail on the Donkey/Hat on the Witch, Magic and a variety of refreshments.

Don't let your children miss this special evening filled with fun and games.

Herman E. Walston, Kentucky State University, Rosenwald Center for Early Childhood Development, Frankfort KY

Halloween Party

On _____, 19__ from _____ to _____.

Games / Songs / Treats

Bring your decorated jack-o'-lantern for the contest!
Come in your costume and join the Pre-K Costume Parade.
Children must come with a parent.

_____

Please tear off and return.

Child's Name_____ Parent's Name _____

I can bring (check one):

    cookies_____ cupcakes_____ donuts_____   cider_____

    fruit_____   nuts_____   raisins_____   chips_____

I can help set up the refreshments:

    yes_____   no_____

Barbara Smolens, Hempstead Public Schools, Pre-Kindergarten, Hempstead NY

Fiesta De Halloween

_____ de octubre de _____ a _____

Juegos Canciones Obsequios

Traiga su linterna hecha de calabaza decorado para el concurso.

Venga disfrazado y tome parte en el desfile de Pre-K.

Los ninos tienen que venir acompanados por sus padres.

_____

Por favor recorte y devuelva.

Nombre del nino_____

Nombre del padre_____

Yo puedo traer (marque uno)

    galletas_____   biscochitos_____   doughnuts_____

    jugo de manzana_____   nueces_____   uvas/pasas_____

Puedo ayudar a preparar la mesa:

    si____   no____

Por favor recuerde que esta fiesta es unicamente para las familias del Pre-K.

Barbara Smolens, Hempstead Public Schools, Pre-Kindergarten, Hempstead NY

About Birthday Snacks And Celebrations

To: All The Nursery School Parents

Birthday Celebrations

_____ has a no-sugar snack policy. We feel that this is important for the physical, dental and mental development of the children. We strongly suggest the accent be put on the happiness of a birthday, the special uniqueness of the birthday child and with the growth and advancement the child has made over the past year.

Concentrate on how the snack is presented (fancy cups, plates, napkins or a goodie-bag), not the actual snack itself. The snack can be special because your child helped prepare it. No cupcakes or cookies, PLEASE! Fruits, vegetables, cheese and crackers, peanut butter on graham crackers, popcorn, pretzels, low sugar cereal, trail mix and apple juice all make GREAT SNACKS. YOU are bringing it — that's what is special to your child.

This year we are trying something new. If you would like to give the school a gift of a storybook on your child's birthday, as part of your child's special day, we will read this book to the class.

It can be presented with your child's name and birthday, written on the inside cover and will be placed in our special birthday book library. Another idea is send some pictures of your child from birth to the present and your child will make a special birthday banner.

We think these ideas along with our traditional birthday crown will help your child feel special. We also feel that we are giving the children a healthy example for sound development.

Thank you for your cooperation.

Margaret Gibson-Adams, The Presbyterian Nursery School on the Green, Bloomfield NJ

Birthday Celebration Invitation

Birthdays are important to children and that is why on _____
                                                                    Date

at _____ we will be celebrating _____ birthday.
        Time   Child's Name

Please let us know if you will be with us.   _____ Yes   _____ No

_____
        Parent Signature

Constance B. Sonnier, Church Point Head Start, Church Point LA

National Children's Book Week

Parents:

   This is National Children's Book Week! To celebrate the importance of children's books, we ask that you assist your child in selecting his/her *favorite* story book to share with the class.

   We will display them on our bookcase during free play and talk about them at circle. Please be sure to mark the book with your child's name to facilitate returns at the end of the week. Thanks for your cooperation.

   Happy Reading.

Cathy Griffin, Dutch Neck Presbyterian Church Cooperative Nursery School, Princeton Junction NJ

Un-birthday Party

Dear Room Parent,

      Our upcoming Un-Birthday Party will be an exciting time here at
_____ as we celebrate **all** of our un-birthdays. The party for your child's group will take place on _____ at
_____.

      To make this a very special time, we need your help. Here's what we'd like you to arrange for the parents of your group to provide:

         1. room decorations — balloons, crepe paper, etc.

         2. nut cups (filled)

         3. festive paper plates, cups and napkins

         4. plastic forks

         5. juice (apple seems to be the best)

         6. a decorated cake saying "Happy Un-Birthday" with 12 candles and matches

         7. a cake server or knife

         8. decorative paper sacks (plainly labeled, one for each child)

         9. a few favors to put in the sacks

Thank you for your willingness to help to make this event a delightful one for each child.

      Sincerely,

Kathie McAfee, Little People Nursery School and Kindergarten, Chico CA

Thanksgiving

Dear Parents,

We will have our Thanksgiving feast in kindergarten on _____, _____. In the spirit of sharing we are asking each child to bring **one small can** (approximately eight ounces) of vegetables from the choices listed here: green beans, potatoes, carrots, corn, whole tomatoes, tomato soup or peas. We will use these cans of vegetables to make our stone soup for our feast. Please send the eight ounce can to school by _____, _____. Any cans of vegetables not used in making our soup will be donated to a food bank for families in need.

Animal Sitters Needed

We are looking for volunteers to care for our classroom pets during the Thanksgiving holidays. If you and your family will be home for the holidays and you would like to care for one of our animals, please return the bottom portion of this note. All of the food and supplies will be provided to care for our pets. If we have more than enough volunteers we will draw names to see who gets the honor. Please return this note by _____, _____ if you are interested.

Thank you.

_____

Animal Sitters

_____ Yes, We will be able to care for one of the classroom pets.

We would like to care for the: _____

Child's Name: _____ Phone Number: _____

Parent's Name: _____

Angela Lowrey, Ditto Elementary, Arlington TX

Holiday Gift Ideas (1)

The Christmas season is very rushed and now highly commercialized. My advice for a gift for your child is *your time.* Your special attention is worth more than any bright present. Take time to make cookies, trim the tree, go for a walk with your child — this they will remember and value in future years.

As far as boxes under the tree — simple is best. Have it be something a child can play with — that needs his or her action or imagination to work.

Some suggestions:

- plastic bottles, sponges, spoons for water play
- sewing cards made from magazine pictures pasted on cardboard
- puzzles
- pasta, macaroni to string as beads
- magnets, magnetic clips to play with on the refrigerator
- paper bag puppets
- bowling pins made from empty milk cartons
- clothes for dress-up
- strainers, colanders, ladles for bath toys
- clothes hanger bent into hoop with Nerf toys to throw through
- flour, water, salt for playdough
- liquid starch and newspaper for papier-mache
- big cartons from new stoves or refrigerators to play in
- empty food cans and boxes for playing store
- table covered with sheet for a playhouse
- thread spools to string
- discarded mail

Have a wonderful holiday!

Andrea Clapper, Child Development Center, SUNY Cobleskill, Cobleskill, NY

Holiday Gift Ideas (2)

Dear Parents,

When you are looking for toys this Christmas, please keep these goodies in mind:

1. lots of paper and pencils
2. easel, drawing paper, scissors, paint
3. clay, playdough
4. magic slate
5. jacks
6. jump rope
7. paddle ball]
8. roller skates
9. hula hoop
10. puzzles
11. checkers
12. ring toss
13. horse shoes
14. chalkboard and chalk
15. books
16. bubbles
17. puppets
18. globe
19. musical instruments
20. wipe-off books
21. flashlight
22. sand box
23. dress-up clothes
24. kaleidoscope

* The best gift — your time and love.

Donna Henry, Portsmouth Catholic School, Portsmouth VA

Kindergarten Holiday Wish List

Dear Parents,

The kindergarten team would like to suggest that rather than purchasing a gift for your child's teacher, you might consider purchasing an item that will be of use to all the kindergarten classes. The list on the bottom of this letter includes items that can be used by students and teachers in the classroom. Two families might consider purchasing an item together for the kindergarten "wish list."

Thank you and happy holidays,

Wish List

- letter file trays
- medium or large soft throw pillows
- child-size plastic painting aprons
- plastic tubs or baskets to store games and manipulatives
- paper towels for cooking and art projects
- plastic mixing bowls for cooking (one set with various sizes)
- adult plastic aprons for cooking and art projects
- round or rectangular tablecloths to cover classroom tables
- child's play tent
- paint cups for the easel
- curtains for our storage shelves
- paint brushes for easel painting
- books (ask teachers for titles)

Angela Lowrey, Ditto Elementary, Arlington TX

Black History Month

Dear Families,

As you may know, February is Black History Month. In working with Pre-K children, our objectives are to:

　　　　a) Develop family pride and

　　　　b) Appreciate and celebrate the likenesses and differences in people.

This includes children becoming aware of black personalities today and in the past. As part of this curriculum, Pre-K will a have a "Black is Beautiful" photo montage in the hall.

Please send in pictures (which will not be returned) of your favorite black personality. Photos of your family would also make a welcome addition. This montage will be displayed in the hall during the month of February. Contributors will be listed beside it.

Please send your photos in a labeled envelope. More than one will be appreciated.

　　　　　　　　Sincerely,

Barbara Smolens, Hempstead Public Schools, Pre-Kindergarten, Hempstead NY

Special Spring Days

One Saturday morning in the spring we have Dad's Day. This is time for fathers (or an appropriate substitute) to join their children in a "mini-day at nursery school." Each dad is asked to bring "show and tell" relating to his work or hobby. The children enjoy preparing the snack for this special occasion.

Mothers are honored guests at special Mother's Day Parties in each class in May. Mothers acting as helping parents on the days of the parties will help *only* during free play and clean-up. All mothers are guests for snack and circle!

Please watch for your child's class calendar, cubby and newsletter for more information.

Cathy Griffin, Dutch Neck Presbyterian Church Cooperative Nursery School, Princeton Junction NJ

Easter Party

Dear Parents,

We will be having an Easter Party on _____. We will be making Easter baskets on another day as one of our art center activities.   Therefore, the children will not need to bring a basket from home. Please send *three* boiled eggs to school with your child on_____ . Please put them in something so that they will not get broken before the children get to school. We will dye the eggs that day for our science learning center activity.

Our Easter holiday will begin on _____. Classes resume on _____.

Have a wonderful Easter.

Sincerely,

Dixie Smith, Ricardo School, Kingsville TX

Pizza Night

Pizza night is this Friday _____ from _____ to _____.

      All children and their families are invited to Pizza Night. It is an opportunity to meet other families, to have supper without cooking and to watch the children play. Come to meet the child that your child is always talking about, or to meet the parents behind the little faces you see in the class every morning and afternoon.

      We ask that each family bring one item — supplies, salad, juice, fruit or dessert. Please sign-up on the sign-up sheet near the door.

      Pizzas will be brought to the Center.

      Cost of the pizzas is: $2 for each adult and $1 for each child. *Please pay in advance* so we have the money for the pizzas.

      We hope you will be able to atend.

      Volunteers needed for set-up and clean-up.

      Please return the bottom portion of this slip with payment of $2 per adult and $1 per child by _____.

_____

Name_____

Number of people in your family coming to pizza night _____

Thank you.

Joyce Stockdill, Silver Spring Child Care Center, Silver Spring MD

Pot Luck Dinner

Dear Parents,

    We will be having a pot luck dinner on _____. The particulars are as follows:

        We will eat in the _____ room.

        We will start at _____.

        We will need to be finished by _____.

- Everyone brings a main dish to feed your group, plus three more people.
- Parents with girls at the Center also bring dessert.
- Parents with boys at the Center also bring salad.
- You may bring the food to the Center that morning or in the evening.

Food that needs to be heated should be here by _____.

Make sure your name is on your containers/dishes.

The Center will supply plates, napkins, forks, cups and drinks. There will be a sign-up sheet in the hallway. If you are planning to come, print your name and the number of people in your group. Please respond by _____.

Remember: You will be responsible for your children during this time. You need to make sure that they don't run around or leave the room. If your child wants to use the playground you must go out and supervise. The Center staff is off-duty and wants to be able to socialize with you.

Pam Humphrey, Takoma Park Day Care Center, Takoma Park MD

Storybook Character Day

As you know, this is National Library Week. Yesterday we visited the library, and the trip was lots of fun! In conjunction with this special week, the classes will have Storybook Character Day on _____, _____. Each student is encouraged to come to school dressed as one of their favorite storybook characters, and to bring the book their character is from. Costumes may be as simple or as elaborate as you want. Please be sure the child's name is on his/her book.

Katy Greenawalt, Bethel Baptist Preschool, Sumter SC

Chapter Eight

Help
Wanted

ABC Collectibles List

Throughout the year, various items from home are needed for projects in your child's classroom. Requests for such articles are posted outside the classroom doors and/or put on the class calendars. Please check for these notices so your child will have the necessary item for a specific project.

Parents are requested to please save the items listed below for class use. Some items are always needed, while others are for special projects. Since storage at the school is limited, please check with your child's teacher before sending in any items. A box or bag at home with the label "nursery school" could serve as a convenient temporary storage place. Everyone's help is needed!

Remember: A "clean disposable" may turn into a "treasured collectible" after your child's special touch has been added through a class project!

The following is a list of useful items for you to save:

A— acorns, appliance cartons, aluminum cups (from Crystal Light and Pillsbury)

B — beans, beads, buttons, belts, big boxes, burlap, baby food jars with lids, berry boxes

C — caps, cardboard, cotton balls, corks, carpet scraps/padding, coffee cans — one pound size, compartmentalized trays, colored cellophane scraps, computer printouts

D — dice, decals, dowels, doilies

E — eggshells, earrings, egg cartons

F — funnels, felt scraps, fabric scraps, frames, floral foil, frosting containers (from Betty Crocker and Pillsbury)

G — gears, gloves, garland scraps, greeting cards

H — hats, hinges, heart-shaped boxes

I — ink bottles, pads, ice-cream cups

J — jewelry, jars, jacks, juice cans — six ounce size

K — keys

L — lids, L'egg's eggs, LeMenu plates

M — meat trays, milk and cream cartons — eight ounce size

N — nails, nuts, newspaper

O — oatmeal boxes, old socks

P — pie pans, postcards, plastic, pinecones, popsicle sticks, pipe cleaners, paper clips, packing cartons

Q — quills, quilt scraps

R — rings, rubber bands, rocks, rope, ribbons, rick-rack, roll-on deodorant jars

S — screws, string, straws, stamps (from magazine sales and holiday seals), six-pack holders, seeds, styrofoam pieces, spools, spice jars, stickers, shells, scoops (from juice mixes) safety pins

T — tubes from paper rolls, tins, trim scraps, travel-size bottles and jars

U — utensils, uniforms

V — valentines, velvet

W — washers, wigs, wool, wood scraps, wallpaper scraps, wire, wipes

X — x-rays

Y — yarn, yardsticks, yogurt cartons

Z — zippers

Cathy Griffin, Dutch Neck Presbyterian Church Cooperative Nursery School, Princeton Junction NJ

Volunteer Assistance Survey

Dear Parents,

As we begin a new year at _____, we realize how greatly our program depends on your volunteer assistance. Without your help, many of our dreams would never be fulfilled!

We ask that you consider the list which we have compiled; however, please feel free to add your own suggestions or comments. We also encourage grandparents as volunteer assistants.

Thank you for your support in so many ways. We look forward to working together during the coming year.

Sincerely,

Please check one or more:

_____playground assistance

_____nursing assistance

_____field trip chaperone

_____special art activity

_____fund-raising

_____classroom aide

_____telephoning

_____other (interests, special talents,tec.)

Best day:

__M __T __W __Th __Fri __Any Day

Signature:

_____

Sister Angela, Sacred Heart Pre-Primary School, Kingston MA

Animal Sitters Needed

We are looking for volunteers to care for our classroom pets during the
_____ holidays. If you and your family will be home for the
holidays and you would like to care for one of our animals, please return the bottom portion of
this note.

We have the following pet(s): _____. All the food
and supplies will be provided to care for our pets. If we have more than enough volunteers we
will draw names to see who gets the honor. Please return this note by
_____, if you are interested.

Thank-you.

_____

Animal Sitters

_____ Yes, we will be able to care for one of the classroom pets.

We would like to care for the: _____

Child's name:_____

Phone number:_____

Parents name:_____

Angela Lowrey, Ditto Elementary, Arlington TX

Help Wanted

Moms   Dads   Grandparents

Excellent part-time opportunity waiting for you in the classroom.

Room moms/dads — to plan games, entertainment, crafts, etc. for our three class parties — Halloween, Christmas, end-of-the-year.

Table helpers — once a week to work with the children in one of the activity areas.

Materials Moms/Dads — Once a month, at home or at school, to make or repair classroom materials.

No experience needed...just a little time to spare and share. The work is rewarding and fun. Exciting environment.

Contact_____.

Kathy Williams, Southwest Surburban Montessori, Palos Park IL

Party Parents

You signed up to help with our _____ party, which we will celebrate on

_____, __/__/__, beginning about _____.

I have asked _____ (Tel:_____)

to coordinate the party.

Other parents helping include:

_____(Tel:_____)

_____(Tel:_____)

See you then.

Jo Ann C. Leist, First Presbyterian Preschool, Smithfield NC

Guide For Helping Parents

1. The helping parent will arrive at least fifteen (15) minutes prior to class time and will not bring any children with him/her other than those enrolled.

2. At the direction of the teacher, the helping parent will assist in setting up the work areas. This procedure will depend on the plans for the day.

3. The primary job of the helping parent is to relieve the teacher of any work other than teaching. The helping parent may be assigned to a particular project, or may be needed to circulate among all of the children offering assistance and encouragement, while *supervising for safety.*

4. Help take children to the bathroom and assist with handwashing. Check the bathrooms for paint marks and wipe out the sinks.

5. Mark all children's work with their name, and help them to place it on newspaper or a drying rack. Assist teachers in placing work in each child's cubby before dismissal.

6. The helping parent will remove paint jars from the easel at clean-up time. Paint, paste and glue containers should be refilled and wiped clean before being put away so that they are fresh for use by the next class.

7. The helping parent will provide refreshments for the day. This shall consist of approximately one (1) gallon of juice or milk and a healthy, creative snack. Helping parent and child will prepare snack for the class, at the direction of the assistant teacher, while the teacher leads group/circle time.

8. At the direction of the teacher, the helping parent will open the playyard and storage closet, remove equipment as directed and return it at the end of the day. *Supervise for safety* on the playground. At least one teacher and the helping parent shall be on the playground at all times.

9. The helping parent will remain after class until all housekeeping chores are completed and all children have left. Before leaving for the day, help the teacher clean and straighten the room.

10. Thank you and enjoy!

Cathy Griffin, Dutch Neck Presbyterian Church Cooperative Nursery School, Princeton Junction NJ